I thoroughly enjoyed reading the book. I cried and I laughed. When I first met Kathy, she was barely able with assistance, to maneuver the stairs up to my office. Our journey together has been one of mutual learning and evolution. I am honored to have been a part of her rehabilitation process.

Dr. Carol Franklyn

Kathy's life has been a challenge for her and her family since the accident, but she has handled Traumatic Brain Injury with grace and determination. Some miracles do happen every day and Kathy has blossomed.

Nurse Linda Proctor RPN

I remember the day you came into my office with your Dad and Mom. You were very sick and today you are a miracle by the Grace of God.

Dr. T. H. Liem

Brain injury is difficult to deal with and there are various deficits with each person. By not accepting what has been dealt, a person will become stuck. You have moved on because you have accepted what you were faced with, and you continue to move forward.

Dr. Albert. P. Ng

UNMASKING POSSIBILITIES

JUST WATCH ME

My 30 year Journey

With Brain Injury

Jan 2024

Your dream doesn't have an expiry date. Take a deep breath and begin again.

Kathy Worotny

Kathy Worotny

with Suzanne De Froy

Thankyou for being part of Helping Hands!! Suzanne De Froy

Disclaimer

This non-fiction memoir highlights real facts, real events, and real people in Kathy Worotny's 30-year recovery journey. Neither the authors or the publisher assumes any responsibility for errors, omissions, or contrary interpretations of the subject matter herein. Any perceived slight of any individual or organization is purely unintentional. Names provided in testimonials and the memory and visitor books have been provided with permission. Documents cited include copies of medical, lawyer, insurance, and other reports given to her family. Unless permission has been given, only the professional's title has been referenced due to privacy laws. Details of Kathy's traumatic brain injury after a devastating car crash in 1993 have been provided in the hope that her experience may benefit victims and their families.

ISBN: 978-1-927591-35-2

About the Cover: The mask was created by Kathy Worotny to illustrate two sides of her life's journey: the past was filled with sunshine; the present is filled with obstacles to overcome. Like a ladybug that goes into hiding during the winter and emerges in the spring, the challenge is continually finding successful ways to survive and thrive. Designed by Walkerville Publishing, Inc.

Book Design:
Walkerville Publishing Inc.
walkerville.com

EST. 1999 WALKERVILLE PUBLISHING

Printed in Canada

Author Contributions:

Kathy Worotny shared her story with the documentation collected by her family to writer and researcher Dr. Suzanne De Froy. As a collaborative effort, both authors have made substantial direct and intellectual contribution to the work and approve this publication.

Statement of Proceeds to BIAWE

Kathy Worotny's involvement in the Brain Injury Association of Windsor Essex has been a major factor in her recovery. Dr. Suzanne De Froy is a board member of this non-profit charitable organization. It is the intention of the co-authors to donate a portion of the book sales so that those who are on their own healing journey from brain injury will also have access to the valuable programs being offered.

"Although I've only known Kathy for a few short years through the Brain Injury Association of Windsor and Essex County (BIAWE), I feel I have known her forever. She exudes vibes of positivity, gratitude, and enthusiasm for life. What is most striking about Kathy is her kindness and willingness to share her knowledge and experience with others. She offers her special skills and talents whenever she is called upon. It is through her drive and determination that she has travelled far on her journey with an acquired brain injury. It is through her spirituality and love that she shares her journey with others. Survivors of a brain injury are given hope and reassurance that life will get better. She is an inspiration for us all to live life to its fullest, with a brain injury or not."

Anna Jurak, Executive Director of Brain Injury Association of Windsor and Essex County

Dedication

This book is dedicated to all victims of acquired brain injury and their Circle of Care, our parents Romeo and Mary Therese Labbe, and James and Ivy DeFroy. Their legacy is faith and encouragement by viewing a world filled with possibilities. They modeled for us how to persevere during difficult times and not get stuck. Their wisdom helped us to bring this project to completion.

CONTENTS

Introduction

When trauma reaches the doorstep of our lives it is not only the victim who suffers, for a ripple effect casts a wide net. Family members, friends, co-workers, medical teams, and communities are affected to varying degrees. Kathy Worotny is a thirty-year survivor of traumatic brain injury who continues to be on a healing journey. Events have been reconstructed, woven through multiple sources including more than 30 medical and professional reports meticulously collected and organized by her father, Romeo Labbe. Weekly notes over a six-year period were graciously provided by her psychologist, Dr. Franklyn. Kathy was encouraged to express herself in personal journals and notebooks. Her scrapbook contains newspaper articles and speeches about the consequences of risk-taking behaviours. Aspects of her story are captured on YouTube videos and her voice is heard as an introduction to courses offered through Brock University. Other voices provide additional insight through an early visitor notebook that contains 123 messages, personal interviews, and over twenty testimonials. Research helped explain the many challenges that were faced by Kathy and her Circle of Care.

Kathy's story is relevant as brain injury is now being considered a worldwide 'silent epidemic'. Long term consequences affect millions and researchers are searching for answers. A significant study followed victims 16 years of age and older over a five-year period who received inpatient rehabilitation services after a primary diagnosis of moderate to severe TBI. The Centre for Disease Control and Prevention posted the startling findings: 22% died, 30% became worse, 22% stayed the same, and only 26% improved. International studies are also raising awareness to this widespread problem. Kathy emerged from death's door to surpass what some of the medical professionals considered "reasonably achievable" by challenging initial predictions that her neurocognitive deficits would be "permanent in nature." It is hoped that those who find themselves dealing with the chaos of brain injury may be able to relate to the hopeful aspects of her story.

This book is divided into six parts. Part I describes events shortly before and after the preventable car crash that occurred when a young man ran a red light. His split-second lapse of judgement resulted in Kathy's world being dramatically changed forever. Resuscitated at the scene, a coupe-contrecoup brain injury caused considerable damage to her brain stem, frontal, and temporal lobes. Initial testing registered 7 on the Glasgow Coma Scale. It took six weeks before emerging into the twilight zone of post-coma unresponsiveness.

Part II describes Kathy's in-hospital rehabilitation experience that began shortly after being stabilized. The transition into higher levels of consciousness took months of patience for everyone in her healing Circle of Care. Kathy had an extensive interdisciplinary team including nurses, personal support workers, therapists, family physicians, allergy specialists, dental surgeons, an ear-nose-throat specialist, endocrinologists, rehabilitation specialists, ophthalmologist, orthopedic specialist, psychiatrist, psychologists, and neuropsychologists. A speech therapist set up a memory notebook nine weeks after the crash to help improve basic language skills and self-awareness. In her own words we can imagine a weaving road of progress and setbacks that marked the beginning of a long road to become the positive resilient person she once was.

Part III illustrates how Kathy navigated the outside world after being released from the hospital as an out-patient. Medical support continued with additional care from personal support workers who arrived to cook, clean, and basically tell her when to wake up, dress, eat, take a bath and finally when to go to bed. Harboring deep resentment that there were many things she could not control, frustration often spilled into intense anger as quickly as flipping a switch. The drastic change in personality typical to TBI was especially difficult for her family. Despite being a former nun, faith and spiritual beliefs dissolved. She was suffering emotionally, physically, and mentally, unable to calm the internal storm of incessant worry about the future. With the help of a compassionate psychologist, Kathy began to slowly adjust to her new changed reality.

Part IV describes a period of transition when the fog started to lift. Professionals explained the extent of her brain injury and suggested that it was in her best interest to accept impairments as a permanent barrier. She would never return to the person she was before the crash. Suicidal thoughts surfaced, raising alarm bells for her psychologist. After slowly acknowledging the cumulative loss, Kathy gave herself permission to grieve. Through a shift in perception, hard work and determination, small steps of progress became milestones. Two concrete goals emerged, opening doors to freedom. She worked hard to have her driver's license reinstated and went back to school in the hopes of returning to teaching. When Kathy started to volunteer, a sense of purpose was sparked by helping others.

Part V is a time of transformation when counselling ended, and the 'old Kathy' became fully integrated into a 'renewed Kathy'. She used her voice to become an advocate for the disadvantaged and often shared her story in small groups and larger audiences in the hopes of preventing risk taking behaviours. The Brain Injury Association of Windsor and Essex County became a port in the storm and presented many enriching opportunities. New relationships enriched Kathy's life with positive healing energy, and she found love and happiness after meeting her husband, Rob.

Part VI offers lessons learned along the journey, with the hope that transcending long lasting cognitive, behavioural, emotional, and physical impairments is possible. Research is revealing the brain's remarkable ability to change and heal itself. By moving beyond limitations, feelings of unworthiness, inferiority, imperfection, and failure are slowly released. Bouncing back to become an active participant in the world depends on an array of factors driven mainly by the victim of brain injury. With the help of empathetic caregivers and medical personnel a victim can be empowered to survive and thrive to achieve optimal health. Kathy found herself on a path that helped her rediscover resilient strengths that led to achieving a quality of life that her family, friends, and doctors call a miracle. Self-awareness improved over time. By finding realistic and sustaining ways to perceive the world Kathy is able to adapt in difficult situations. It is hoped that through her story, others will be able to discover their internal wisdom and achieve personal fulfillment and happiness despite adversity. It has been an honour to walk beside Kathy in the unravelling of her 30-year journey.

Suzanne De Froy, EdD
Co-author

Part I

The Beginning of the Journey

"A dove struggling in a storm grows stronger than an eagle soaring in sunshine"
Matshona Dhliwayo

The morning of Ash Wednesday, February 24th, 1993, I was in a head on car crash that started a miraculous journey away from death's door. The events leading up to that day are sacred because the old Kathy died that day. Resting deep in my long-term memory are feelings of joy, love, and happiness that as a renewed Kathy, I am still able to recall. The positive energy from these memories helped rekindle the resilience I needed to move past the traumatic suffering that came my way. Many lessons were learned before I ultimately realized that it is up to me to decide what I am going to do with my pain. Acceptance of life altering changes is not easy, but I have passed through a tumultuous 30-year storm to find the healing energy of love, peace, contentment, and gratitude.

The week before my car crash, we were preparing for my brother Phil's wedding. My sister Pauline and I were so excited to be bridesmaids. It was a time filled with happy family get-togethers at my parents' home. The day finally arrived, and I can still see Phil kneeling at the altar beside Cathy, his beautiful happy bride. We didn't know that his best man had written 'HELP' on the bottom of one shoe and 'ME' on the other. As my brother greeted the guests outside the church, one of his friends told him to read the bottom of his shoes. I still remember the surprised look on his face while we were having a good laugh. Being with our close-knit family and good friends, the weekend remains a very happy memory.

Phil and Cathy's bridesmaids

As Phil and his new bride left for their honeymoon in Cuba, the rest of us settled back into our usual routines. We were looking forward to more family visits. Aunt Julie was flying in from Thunder Bay on Tuesday evening and my cousin's wife Sharon Forgeron was arriving on Wednesday afternoon to attend a speech pathologist conference in Detroit. They made plans to stay at my house while I went to teach at St. Anne's High School in Tecumseh. To me teaching was more than a job. It was my life's vocation – a calling to serve. I received my qualifications when I was a nun with the Sisters of the Holy Names of Jesus and Mary (SNJM). I loved my students and the St. Anne's community. During my first five years teaching religion I became very concerned that several of my students struggled with reading and writing. I brought my concerns to John Staley, our principal. He was able to initiate a life skills program and appointed me as the teacher-coordinator. Every day was an adventure during the next seven years. I worked with a team of educators who were dedicated to meet the unique needs of our students. During that time, I left the convent and became an associate with the SNJM community.

Being flexible was easy for me. I thrived on being creative in solving problems and coping with change. There always seemed to be one or more unforeseeable circumstances that students or staff would bring at the start of each day. Saying things could be unpredictable is an understatement as each student in the program had needs that were considered exceptional. We had social workers, psychologists, nurses, occupational and speech therapists visiting us regularly. Coordinating appointments within the school day was part of my responsibility and changes often had to be made on the fly.

I liked to get an early start and be on the road by 7:00 a.m. Starting early helped alleviate stress. I made sure there was an organized plan for the day's routine. I wanted to do all I could to ensure a smooth transition as students moved from their homes into our school community. Our students arrived at 7:50 a.m. and even though it was a hectic time to get everyone settled we encouraged one another to start the day on a positive note. I used a huge white board to facilitate additions and changes. Every student had a daily journal as a means for clear communication between the educational assistants, parents and at times the group homes where some of the students lived. We never sent a student home without a comment on how the day went so the parents and caregivers knew what to expect. We were very aware that activities or negative interactions at school can influence mood changes and could be detrimental to a student's well-being.

Designing curriculum in a life skills pilot program was a real-life experiment. A primary goal was to provide opportunities for students to learn how to become independent and care for themselves. Novel aspects supplemented the traditional curriculum including food preparation, showering, and personal hygiene. Building bridges to break down feelings of isolation meant that students needed to feel connected. Depending on functioning levels, I worked with classroom teachers to find creative ways to integrate our students into the natural flow of our school community. Our students also volunteered to launder uniforms for different sports teams and it was good to see how they felt their contributions were appreciated.

Learning basic math skills was part of our curriculum. Students were taught the fundamentals of money, especially coin and bill recognition.

Mondays became regular banking days at our community's Caisse Populaire. Each student was encouraged to bring a bit of cash and we would walk to the bank and make a deposit into their account. I also wanted to prepare students for life after high school, so I reached out to the business community to find suitable co-op placements. Torino's Restaurant provided a chance for my students to learn kitchenhand skills. They assisted the chef with food preparation and learned how to maintain a clean area by washing utensils, dishes, pots, and pans. At Tecumseh Daycare they prepared snacks and cleaned up after children. Home Hardware and Zehr's Supermarket provided opportunities for my students to organize and stack shelves.

Main-stream student volunteers became peer helpers, which was a key component to our success. On Tuesday, February 23rd, the day before the collision, I brought four peer helpers to Burger King to show my gratitude for all their help. I still remember our laughter as they reminisced about my playful antics. At Hallowe'en I would paint my face green and dress up in a witch costume and I also loved being a jolly Santa Claus at Christmas assemblies. It was an exciting time as our program evolved becoming a model for other high schools at our board. Thirty years later I feel blessed to have so many happy long-term memories that are still with me. Before Ash Wednesday I could never have imagined that in a fleeting instant I would be literally walking in the shoes of my students.

Split Second Lapse of Judgement

Everything that happened from noon at Burger King on Tuesday, until six weeks later while I was in a coma is non-existent. This condition is known as pre-traumatic or retrograde amnesia. In lay person's terms, it is a loss of memory for a period before a brain injury occurs. Periods of broken memories remain, as my brain protected me from the overwhelming stimulation. It has been so hard to accept that some memories are simply gone, and it has become important to reconstruct key events. I have relied on medical reports and the recollections from my family, friends, and colleagues to fill in the gaps leading up to and immediately following the crash.

Aunt Julie said I left my house later than usual that morning because I took the time to show her where things were in my kitchen so she could feel at home. My educational assistants were aware that my routine might be a little different. A bank receipt was found in my car indicating that I changed my route. Taking E. C. Row Expressway, I needed to make a left-hand turn at

Lesperance Road. Oncoming traffic had a red light, and I had a green arrow. As I was in the middle of my turn, the driver of a westbound Chevrolet S10 Blazer ran the red light. My car was hit on the passenger side, causing it to spin and slide off the road coming to rest on the grass next to the graveyard. In that fateful moment of haste, my life was changed forever.

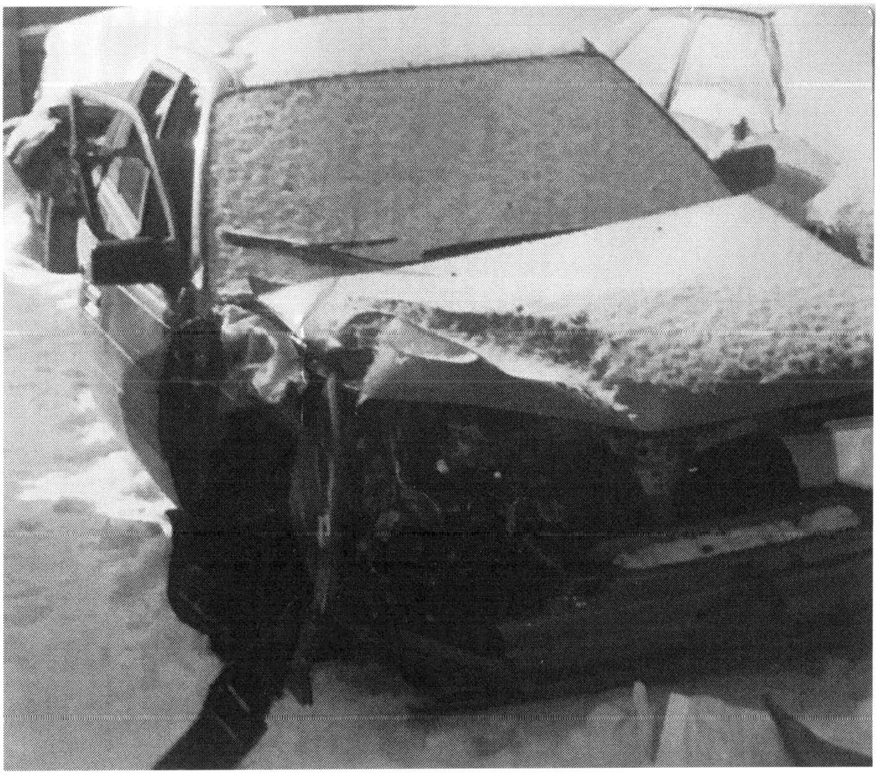

Car crash, February 24th 1993

One of my students was on his way to his co-op placement at Home Hardware. When he recognized my damaged car, he ran back to school to let people know. My principal Mr. Staley immediately rushed to the scene and saw my head in the glove compartment. My feet were hanging outside the passenger door. He watched in shock as the paramedics lifted me out of the car and pumped my chest before taking me away in the ambulance. News swept through our close-knit school community quickly. My colleague Pat Mulvey still remembers how she felt that day:

> *On that cold February morning in 1993, I remember hearing the news of Kathy's terrible car accident. Kathy's vehicle had been hit so close to school. Shock and disbelief were the feelings that overwhelmed me at the time... How and why? How could*

such a terrible fate befall such a young and vibrant person? Why Kathy, of all people? On that Ash Wednesday, the entire school was saddened, and we offered prayers for Sister Kathy as we did for the long days, weeks and months that followed.

My Healing Circle of Care

Arriving unconscious at Hotel Dieu Hospital the nurses in the emergency room noted I could not respond to simple verbal commands such as blinking or moving parts of my body. My responses registered 7 on the Glasgow Coma Scale, indicating severe brain injury. I was immediately intubated and administered the drugs Versed and Mannitol. My parents received the phone call from the police at 8:30 a.m. When they arrived at Hotel Dieu Hospital they were led into a private room by a pastoral minister where the ambulance attendants gave them my belongings. I was wearing my white coat and all my clothes were cut in half, covered in blood. My glasses were broken, and my watch stopped working at 8:05 a.m.

Fear and uncertainty mounted because they were unable to see me. The cat scan was not working so I was rushed to another hospital. The chaos made my parents frantic with worry. Upon return to Hotel Dieu, a Richmond Bolt was drilled into my right frontal skull bone to monitor intracranial pressure and the danger of worsening brain injury. When my parents were finally able to see me, they said my face was three times its normal size and there were stitches on the top of my head. I was attached to all kinds of monitoring devices. Blood was found in my right external auditory canal. I had bone fractures in my upper jaw, right foot, and basal part of my skull. My right knee was shattered, and my tibia bone was broken. Extensive bruising covered my entire body.

When interviewed my mother said, *"On that day I was living a horrible nightmare and I thought it was the end of her."* My father never talked about that day. Our family was still grieving the loss of my youngest sister Myra who was only 26 years old when she died from a rare blood disorder two years before. All they could think about was gathering the family together to get through another crisis. Pauline was notified through her employer and word was sent to my brother Phil who was on his honeymoon in Cuba.

Hours dragged on as they sat in the waiting room with my principal John Staley and my dear friend Sister Emma who is a nun in the Sisters of the Holy Name of Jesus and Mary community. A neurosurgeon arrived to say that difficult decisions would have to be made if there wasn't a change in my condition within 48 hours. They heard the terrifying words that implied there was a real possibility of "pulling the plug." These three words stand out from all the conversations in the early hours after being notified. Losing another daughter was incomprehensible. The rest of that first week was a dreadful blur. Gratefully, cousin Sharon was staying at my house with Aunt Julie, and they kept everyone in our extended family circle informed:

> *What a shock it was when your parents arrived at the train station to pick me up and told me of your catastrophic accident that morning ...I immediately felt that I should not be there complicating your family's lives further. They must have been in shock, but they did not skip a beat in making me feel welcome ...they shared details about your care and progress and visiting you in the hospital was so emotional. To hold your swollen hand was such a privilege. I still tear up to think of it. As a Speech-Language Pathologist, I learned that it is vital to assume understanding, so I talked to you, encouraged you, kissed your forehead as I moved around the life support equipment.*
>
> *I knew the Labbe family are no strangers to tragedy, having already lost your sister Myra so suddenly and at such a young age. And now, another daughter's prognosis for recovery and even survival was so grave. Your family understood this but never visibly lost hope. How wonderful it was at such a frightening time to be with people of strong faith where prayer was evident and welcomed.*

My mother remembers the numbing feelings of helplessness, "*It was the countless prayers that held us together to face grave uncertainty. Everyone gave us hope that you would survive.*" Recollections have helped me realize that my entire family was in crisis. The outpouring of heart-felt support by everyone who knew us was overwhelming. The loving circle of concern expanded beyond expectations. From the first moment I was wheeled into the emergency room my family came to be on first name basis with the hospital staff. They quickly realized that the road to recovery would be filled with uncertainty as I was still unconscious when I was transferred from the Emergency Room to the Intensive Care Unit at the Lead Trauma Centre in Windsor. Questions concerning prognosis seemed to hang in the air as clear answers were avoided.

Traumatic Brain Injury

Generally, predictions are difficult to make in the days and months following a brain injury. In deep coma, my eye movement was unnoticeable for four weeks. There were so many variables involved in the healing process that would affect my mental, physical, emotional, and spiritual well-being, some easily diagnosed, others yet to be revealed. Years later, a clinical psychologist reviewed my medical history for insurance purposes starting from the day I was admitted. He noted that among my injuries from the crash, I sustained a closed traumatic brain injury (TBI) caused from a coupe-contrecoup blow to my head. As my body was thrown out of my seat, my brain ricocheted back and forth on the inside of my skull across the sharp bony ridges that hold the brain in place. This caused bleeding, bruising, and tearing of brain tissue. The sudden acceleration and deceleration of the skull severely affected multiple areas of my brain. I was diagnosed with *"diffuse axonal injury from the motor vehicle accident with no indication of an extracranial hematoma."* In other words, I had multiple neurological problems that affected my physical and mental wellbeing without evidence of bleeding from blood vessels located outside of my skull.

Traumatic brain injury is classified as a mechanical injury to the neurons and blood vessels of the brain at the time of trauma that disrupts normal brain function and mental processes. Considerable damage occurred to areas of my brain stem, temporal and frontal lobes. Briefly, the brainstem is at the back of the skull that sends messages to the rest of our bodies to regulate balance, breathing, heart rate and relays information from the body to the brain. Temporal lobes sit behind the ears and are associated with processing sensory information, understanding language, encoding memory, and managing emotions. The frontal lobes are the largest part of the brain, located directly behind the forehead and are the most common region of traumatic brain injury. These coordinate voluntary movement, the forming of memories, and a collection of cognitive skills such as the capacity to problem solve, plan, organize, initiate, and self-monitor acceptable social interaction through empathy and expressive language. Working in conjunction with the central nervous system these three parts of the brain have a role in managing and controlling responses to external stimuli. Indirectly it was noted that I had secondary inflammation and edema (swelling).

The news was devastating. Except for one or two small parts of the nervous system we stop making new neurons before birth. I would never return to my pre-injury condition because once neurons are dead and the connections severed, they cannot be reattached. The good news today is the medical world recognizes that the brain has the capacity to heal itself by rewiring and growing new pathways among the billions of still healthy neurons. This amazing breakthrough in the evolving medical research on brain plasticity suggests that the likelihood of bouncing back after trauma improves through on-going learning, healing experiences, and rebuilding resilience factors that may be suppressed due to injury. It is a lifelong process! A hopeful outlook begins by consciously adopting a positive attitude and perspective (Doidge, 2007).

Caution is raised to consciously manage the residual effects from increased anxiety, stress, and anger. Otherwise, not only will improvement to brain activity in areas of attention span, cognitive flexibility and creative thinking become inhibited, negative pathways can become further entrenched. In other words, once defeatist attitudes, habits, or beliefs become firmly established, change is very difficult or unlikely. It took me a very long time to realize how important it is not to dwell on what you can't do because moving forward requires focusing on what you can do.

The Visitor Book

My parents strongly believed in the healing energy of love. They recognized I also had post traumatic amnesia causing serious memory limitations. As people beyond our immediate family circle came to visit five weeks after the crash, they brought a simple lined notebook and left it at the side table beside my bed with a pen secured to the binding. What started out as a record of dates and names became a diary of what the doctors never witnessed. I am very grateful for this foresight. One hundred and twenty-three messages over a sixteen-week period were written to me at a time that I could never have guessed would mean so much today. Blank spaces that my memory loss created have been bridged. There are some things I remember clearly. Some are fuzzy and so many moments are lost as I have absolutely no recall at all. Several entries have moved me deeply as I go back in time to try and reconstruct gaps in my memory.

Despair and feelings of helplessness were met with deep compassion as I slowly moved through the various phases of recovery into full consciousness. Abundant encouragement flowed on the pages for there was so much hope that the old Kathy would one day return to them. Four weeks after the crash, on March 23rd, 1993, the nurses allowed two visitors into my room who said they were family. Carol Staley, an educational assistant in my life skills program drew a smiling sun in my book and wrote, *"Hang in there Kath! We love you!"* Andrea Leon, a peer-helper, and student of mine wrote, *"I know you will be back to your old cheerful self in no time."* Visitors from my school community relayed hopeful news. Their impressions help me realize the healing energy of being in community as expressed by my friend and teaching colleague Arlene Veitch:

> *The day of your accident there were shockwaves all over the school. Most of us could not believe that it was true ... and we prayed for you day after day. When we were finally able to visit you in the hospital, I was overwhelmed. I saw you in the big white hospital bed --- and you could not talk --- you could barely open your eyes --- and I was overcome with this feeling of dread --- and I thought that was going to be the last day I saw you alive. I remember crying all the way home, saying goodbye to you in my prayers. Then slowly we heard you were making a miraculous day by day slow progress.*

Slow Progress Begins

Thankfully, I can make connections today through the prayerful voices captured in the written word, which has been very helpful in my ongoing healing process. I was receiving the energy of hope when words had no meaning and comprehension was beyond my grasp. I have been told many times that it is a miracle that I survived the crash after being resuscitated at the scene.

During week 6, I started responding to my surroundings. I mumbled *"Dad"* and *"Mom."* At that moment, my Dad left the room crying. When I was still in a minimally conscious state, my parents could only stand by watching helplessly as I pulled the tubes out of my nose and arms forcing the nurses to strap me to the sides of the bed. Slowly I entered a state of confusion and disorientation, unmindful of myself or my surroundings. When I was able to follow basic instructions, I was moved from the Intensive Care Unit to the Neurology Floor. When I tried to speak, the words were unclear, and I never finished a complete sentence. I called dear friends by names that did not make sense. Sister Emma, was there from the very beginning and recorded some of my first muddled utterances in my visitor book, *"Very dirty glasses ...I don't know ...Mom works very hard ...Love you lots!"*

Emerging from being totally unresponsive into higher levels of consciousness took months of patience for everyone in my healing circle of care. Listening, being able to talk, and developing the ability to understand were milestones in my recovery. Shortly after my vital signs were stabilized, an orthopedic surgeon operated to repair the broken tibia bone in my shattered right leg. The bone had to be broken and set with a plate and pins that were not removed until three years later. Learning to walk again would be a significant hurdle in my healing journey. I continue to suffer from this injury and every day I carefully survey my surroundings and take special care not to fall.

Mention of my progress and loving support flowed every day on the pages of my visitor book. Word of my crash travelled quickly, and 'non-family' visitors who claimed they were family, managed to see me. Colleen Travers, an old friend I met when I was eighteen came to visit me from Michigan and wrote, *"Hi Kathy! We heard you talk quite a bit today. You drank from a cup of water twice, and said, 'I love you' to me (Thanks) and even tried to whistle. I will be here in the morning if they'll let me in. Bless you."* She returned the next day at 8:30 a.m. writing, *"I visited before returning home Kathy. You and I had breakfast (ha ha). You ate all your jello and looked calmer this morning. I love you and will see you soon."*

During week 7 more visitors came to visit from my St. Anne's High School community. Educational Assistant, Chris Butler wrote, *"Kathy, you were so talkative today. I felt like a million bucks when I left. I love you, smiley face."* I was known for my collection of clowns and another Educational Assistant, Joyce Carter wrote, *"Hi Kathy. I really enjoyed our visit. Glad to see you still have your sense of humour. PS Hope the clown gives you some pleasurable moments!"* Annette Lozon, a retired guidance counsellor who worked with me had just returned from her trailer in Florida writing, *"At last I am finally here Kath – It is so good to see you. God how I prayed in Florida! You had tons of people praying down there for you and I so wanted to see you again. I'll be back. You look great and I love you dearly."* The love, compassion, and prayerful encouragement from my St. Anne's community became spiritual nourishment, and I am forever grateful.

Simone Couture, a nurse in the hospital and former nun in my SNJM community wrote, *"Hi Kathy. You were sleeping when I first arrived. I stood by looking at you, loving you and praying. You looked up and smiled at me, so I began talking to you. You said several words that I could not make out and that's okay. You are talking, that is what is important, will come again towards the morning. Love you."* She checked on me again at 5:00 a.m.

writing, *"You spoke a lot to me. I am so happy and proud of you. Keep up the good work. Love you."* Simone was a link to God for many times she came and visited during her breaks and always said a hope-filled prayer. Friends who were just like family also stopped by and recognized the anger that was starting to surface, *"Today we took you outside. You look a lot better than you did last week. Your speech is much clearer and faster today. I curled your hair a little. I am coming back on Sunday to take you to the chapel, so you better be good, Love Bob and Cindy Quenneville."*

Patricia Mulvey, a teacher colleague recalled how I was before the crash, *"Always smiling and amiable, Kathy was a breath of fresh air in the staff room and in the halls. She taught her students well with her positive example."* Yet there were many mixed messages reminding me to behave because I became the very opposite to how I was before the crash. As I became increasingly alert, drastic changes to my personality began to emerge, especially bouts of anger and in general I was very irritable. I now realize that part of the brain regulates our inhibitory responses (suppressing an inappropriate automatic response or action). When we lose full self-awareness, destructive instincts can emerge full force causing harm to our relationships. This became a major hurdle I needed to overcome.

During these early weeks of recovery, I have often imagined myself as a ladybug that went into hiding during the darkest days of winter. When a ladybug finds a safe spot to hide in, they will survive, emerging into the light of spring. I now have a small tattoo of a ladybug on my arm as a reminder of surviving that horrific day. I emerged from death's door into a long period of recovery and renewal to live a miracle. Looking back at visitor entries written while I was moving in and out of coma has been a gift for I have warm feelings of truly being loved.

Ladybug
(photo courtesy Nicole Thibert)

Part II

Rehabilitation

"You may encounter many defeats, but you must not be defeated. In fact, it may be necessary to encounter defeats so you can know who you are, what you can rise from, how you can still come out of it."
Maya Angelou

Over the past 30 years, I have tried to understand the complexity of recovering from traumatic brain injury, so I don't stumble back down the slippery slope into hopelessness. I extend the gift of hope for recovery and offer what I have learned from the different phases of recovery so others will not feel alone in the despair. I entered the rehabilitation phase when I was able to respond to simple instructions. Healing from brain injury is a huge undertaking with many trials and tribulations. Commitment and extremely hard work will be required by the victim who will need support and companionship from a healing circle of care.

My parents obtained power of attorney so my life could move forward legally. There were many professionals in my medical team taking care of my needs including an orthopedic surgeon, an internist, urologist, psychiatrist, therapists, and social workers. Priests and chaplains also visited me regularly when my spirituality was in turmoil. After dedicating so many years of my life in service I couldn't figure out how God would let this happen. Although I never returned to my pre-injury self and there have been devastating pitfalls that I had to overcome, I made significant gains eventually creating a place in the world for a renewed Kathy.

One Day at a TIme

Seven weeks after the crash I was moved to IODE Rehabilitation Hospital in an agitated and confused state. Linda Proctor, a registered practical nurse recounts that day: *"Kathy became an inpatient on the Rehab Unit in April '93. She arrived on a stretcher and was not "a happy camper".* The transport personnel, just looked at us and said, *"Good Luck!"* We found out that in her delusion she thought she was going home, but that was not the case. My Mom wrote in my visitor book, *"Kathy is at Windsor Western. She says she is in her apartment. She says it's October. We talk about what is happening today, Wednesday, April 7th, Holy Week."*

Shortly after I arrived, the first extensive neuropsychological testing of many was conducted over two days by a student in the Clinical Psychology Program. I wanted to cooperate and remember feeling important being the Centre of attention but then became frustrated. The findings were included in a report prepared by a neuropsychologist dated July 15th, 1993, stating:

> *Overall, the results indicate Kathy's verbal skills fall between low to below average range with a significant weakness in her production of words during more complex tasks. These findings would suggest that Kathy may experience difficulty when required to express herself, as well as experiencing some difficulty when required to comprehend more complex verbal statements or instructions. Given Kathy's reported level of prior education and her reported career as a special education teacher, it is probable that her present level of verbal functioning is below her capacities prior to the reported accident. These factors could combine to result in Kathy feeling considerable frustration and/or anxiety when required to either produce or interpret verbal information. It could also interfere with her ability to express her feelings or needs at any given time, which would result in further frustration.*

Because the report was prepared by a doctor who interpreted the test results, I could not reconcile the findings written by someone I never met. I was really ticked off because I felt she was saying that I was 'stupid'. I never used such a derogatory term about impairments before my crash, but that is exactly what I thought. The feelings of being defeated lingered for a very long time. According to this professional, the chance to experience the joy of teaching was slim. I harbored deep resentment that the crash took so much from me.

Bewitching Time

As a result of frontal lobe injury, the darker side of my personality change became more pronounced, and I gained a wide reputation for aggressively lashing out. Evening was my bewitching time. I could not sleep as sleeping pills seemed to have the opposite effect leaving me groggy during the day and awake when I should have been sleeping. Often, I watched TV and called my parents even at 3 a.m. as I had no concept of time. My brother's sister-in-law, Sue Baker, worked the midnight shift as the switch board operator. Sometimes I would call to talk to Sue when I was on a rampage, planning how to escape. She often used her break to visit me and calm me down.

Once I called 911 demanding an ambulance saying, *"You got me here. Come and take me home ...just leave me on my porch and somebody will come to let me back into my house."* The person on the phone tried to calm me down and when they said they were unable to help me, I just hung up and called 911 back again for police assistance. This time I said, *"I am being held hostage and need you to come and arrest all the f***** nurses."* I was assured they would investigate. The head nurse later told me what happened and that the police did in fact report they had a patient in distress. She simply replied, *"Yes, and we know who it is."* The next day my phone was disconnected and if I wanted to talk to my parents, I had to go through the nurses' station, which was right across from my room. They had no trouble listening to me scream at them in outrage.

News travelled fast and I reluctantly had to make amends. Sue tried to remind me to be socially appropriate and once she wrote in my visitor's book: *"I'm glad you apologized to the nurses. I will see you again on the weekends and earlier if I can. I'm glad to see you are eating more."* But the shame of my actions was short lived because I lacked empathy. In my mind, I had the right to be indignant and say exactly what I was thinking. I became so out of control that the nurses placed me on a 'behaviour contract'. My phone was taken out of my room for six weeks. When I gained my phone privileges back, only certain numbers could be accessed – all others were blocked.

Aside from my mother, Sister Emma became the go-to person when the nurses could no longer deal with me. They would call her to come to the hospital so she could calm my aggression. All she had to do was walk into my room, cross her arms, and not say a word. When I was really in a non-compliant mood, she pulled back my curtains, put toothpaste on my toothbrush, filled the sink with warm water, then handed me a facecloth.

Gently but firmly, she told me *"It's time for you to get up and get dressed."* Sister Emma's positive energy and kindness had a calming effect on my troubled spirit and her thoughtfulness helped me regain a sense of dignity. One day in April she arranged for an outside hairdresser to come to the hospital to wash, cut and set my hair. She even obtained a parking pass for my parents through the SNJM community. Her compassionate spirit uplifted the long shadow of misery that threatened hope and optimism.

My Memory Notebook

Cognitively I had many deficits, so rehabilitation took months to re-learn basic skills. Misery settled in when I was reminded that in a fraction of seconds, I went from being a life skills teacher to become a life skills student. I had to re-learn how to talk, read, write, walk, feed, and dress myself. I also had to re-learn reasoning and basic judgement skills. My broken memory caused by post traumatic amnesia contributed to my emotional pain and suffering. My speech language therapist introduced another strategy to help restore essential cognitive functions. She took the time to update everyone by writing in my visitor book, *"Saw Kathy for therapy today and talked about using a memory book. I said that the occupational therapist will get Kathy a bag to keep the book in for her wheelchair and a special pen attachment to make writing easier."*

The simple lined notebook captured important activities of the day and milestones in my recovery. On April 23rd I made my first attempt to print four goals addressing disrespectful behaviour. It was my sister Pauline who added, *"Calm down and work on being nice with the FAMILY."*

Pauline came to visit me almost every day filled with good intentions to ground me into an alternative reality. Much later in my recovery we talked about the day when she tried to help me realize I wasn't getting out of the hospital right away. I had no concept of time and flew into a rage. My sister had to develop her own strategies on how to deal with me and one of them was to simply walk away. Her sudden departure made me stop and before long, I calmed down forgetting what it was all about that triggered my anger. When she came back, we both cried because we wanted to get along, but we were not sure how to deal with my anger and frustration. I did not know I was living the saying, *'We hurt the ones we love the most.'*

As I tried to painstakingly follow instructions, I was encouraged to list small accomplishments in my memory book. Each week I had a schedule

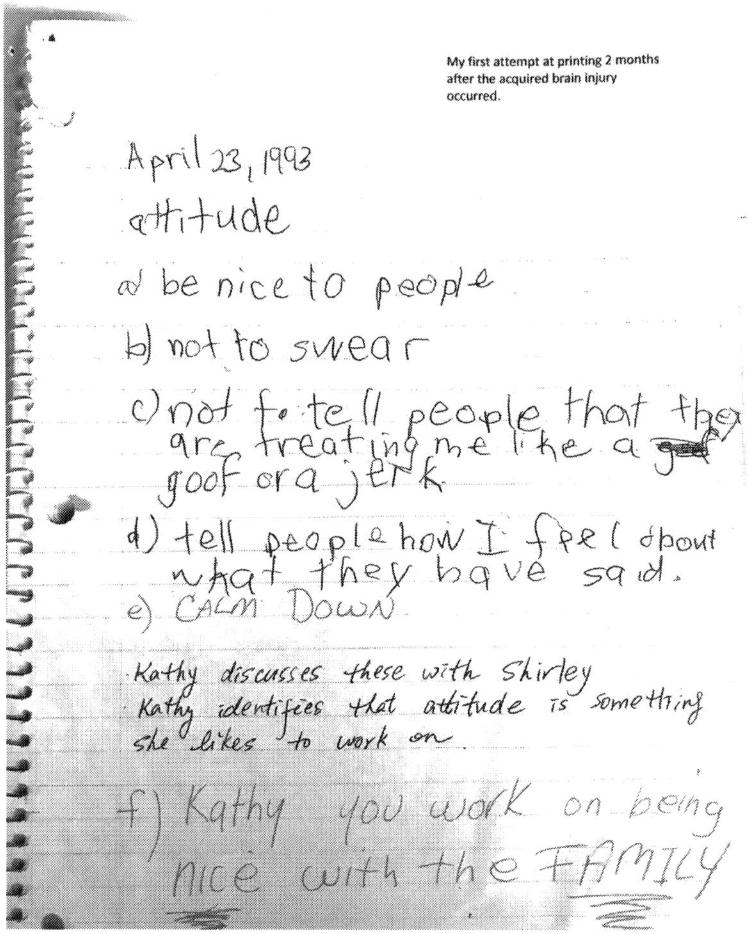

My first attempt at printing 2 months after the acquired brain injury occurred.

April 23, 1993

attitude

a) be nice to people

b) not to swear

c) not to tell people that they are treating me like a goof or a jerk

d) tell people how I feel about what they have said.

e) CALM DOWN

Kathy discusses these with Shirley

Kathy identifies that attitude is something she likes to work on.

f) Kathy you work on being nice with the FAMILY

First attempt at printing in memory book

with occupational, speech and physio therapists and I briefly recorded what we did each day. It provided another link for my healing circle of care by letting everyone know what was going on around me beyond telephone calls and the reams of reports the medical staff had to fill out. Along with the overlapping timeline in the visitor book, valuable clues illustrate my recovery. Thankfully, obstacles were identified, and a trajectory of progress as well as periods of relapse have not been lost in time or hidden away in a record vault.

The Prison

In my broken mind the IODE rehabilitation hospital was a prison. I was on everyone's schedule and at their beck and call. Nurses came in and out of my room to announce the time to get up, when to eat, when to take my pills, when to go to therapy and appointments. One of my most unpleasant memories is the stress caused by wearing diapers. I will never forget the feelings of embarrassment and shame. To me it was undignified and unacceptable. In therapy I learned how to safely slide over from a wheelchair and sit on a raised mat, a chair, or the toilet. So, the necessity to wear diapers should have come to an end. But my nurses had a nightly routine that included emptying my bladder with a catheter then putting the diaper on.

I could not understand the broader reality of nursing workload. All I wanted was their support to get to the bathroom and I could do the rest. Long periods of waiting increased my frustration. When the nurses would not answer my call bell, I would get so humiliated and upset at myself because necessity made me release into the diaper. I had no alternative. Then I had to wait to be changed, which became increasingly annoying. I became focused on getting out of my situation. One night I managed to unlatch the diaper and painfully, wiggle out of it. I threw it onto the floor beside my bed with thoughts, *"I'll show them ...Don't want to answer my bell? So now you must deal with that!"* My distorted perception was bent on revenge.

When I finally stopped needing diapers, I developed problems of urinary incontinence. I underwent a cystoscopy of my bladder followed with regular urine samples being taken. The findings indicated that there was nothing physically wrong. I was put on a bathroom schedule but when I felt the urge, I was often told it was not time for me to go so I had to wait ... again. I believe it was a simple matter of being under extreme stress. Even today, when I perceive I'm in a stressful situation, the urge to go to the bathroom surfaces. To make matters worse I also developed yeast infections, treated with antibiotics. I had to have cream inserted vaginally by the nurses leaving me embarrassed. I would cry long into the night when they left.

There are no words to express the extent of my desperation to escape. I did not have the cognitive capacity or filter to stop myself from saying what came into my mind. I was unable to regulate what I said, often swearing profusely to make a point. Sister Gloria Drouillard wrote, *"Hey Kathy. Glad you can express the fact that you are pissed off! This shows definite progress. At least you are not afraid to show your feelings. Keep trying! Don't give up and get pissed off at the right things."* I was in desperate need of emotional healing that was beyond traditional medical treatment.

My Family: The Heart and Soul of my Healing Circle of Care

Everyone who supported me became part of my ever-widening circle of care. Victims of a car crash are caught in a net that mercilessly encircles family, friends, and many people in their community. Continuously advocating for me, my family never gave up despite my abuse. My Dad came every night but never wrote in my notebooks. He too was traumatized and up to the day Dad passed on he was unable to speak about the early days, simply saying, *"It was all a nightmare, and I can't remember much of it."* My Mom on the other hand says she has a clear memory of the time I was in the hospital. She was my vigilant advocate constantly fighting for me to ensure the medical plan being implemented would always be in my best interest. Both of my parents shared their hope and positive attitude everywhere they went. My cousin Marlene Landry who lives in Nova Scotia was kept informed about my progress:

> *"The very two people who gave Kathy the feisty determination were working tirelessly to ensure that she was receiving the best care possible. Her parents ensured she was surrounded by medical professionals who had a positive attitude and not one of defeat… fighting for her when she could not speak for herself and fight they did!*

Dad drove Mom every day or she took the bus. She only wrote in my visitor notebook a couple of times hoping the nurses would tell me that she was there while I was sleeping. On May 6th she wrote, *"I was here at 1:30 but you were gone for tests in the next building. See you soon, Mom."* She was on her own mission to see me through this difficult time and do everything she could to help me get better. Like Sister Emma, regaining my dignity was also important to her so she would be there early in the morning to take care of my personal needs. She always made sure I got dressed and brushed my hair. To the relief of the staff, she often accompanied me to therapy sessions. I responded much better when she was there because I didn't want her telling me to behave.

My brother Phil and his new wife Cathy visited often. As soon as they returned from their honeymoon, they brought me a Caribbean doll that I kept close to me the entire time I was in the hospital. Phil always walked in with a small present in his hand, usually a Tim Horton's coffee or a pop with a straw. It was his special way to try and put a smile on my face. My sister often left words of encouragement or a message for others to read, *"Kathy you are special. You are doing good with everything. I love you. You have touched my life and I miss you. Kathy did excellent. She will get out soon. Love Pauline."*

Trust Issues

Despite all the good intentions and generous effort, I had major trust issues with just about everyone. Pauline told me that while she was washing my hair one day, I thought she was hurting me on purpose. When I erupted into a swearing tirade, she walked out of the room leaving me with a wet head. When she returned five minutes later it was as if she had not even been there. I was exhibiting rapid changeability typical for TBI. I had no idea that she had been washing my hair or that I was furious at her just a few minutes before. To help ease the tension, a speech-language pathologist spoke to my family and explained that the brain injury overshadows what I would say.

It was no secret that I distrusted most of the staff and gave very bad names to some of the nurses. My uncle Nick and his wife Mary stopped by and wrote, *"Dear Kathy, Nice to see you in good spirits. You are looking well. It seems you have a problem with Miss Saigon and other staff. You must try harder. They are here to help you."* My brother-in-law Norman Isherwood wrote, *"This is the first time I have written anything in this book. I have been here every day since you were admitted. You are doing a hell of a lot better now and have started to tell me off too."*

Our extended family and close friends were always anxious to find out if there was progress in my recovery. As someone paid a visit, they would pass along the most recent news. On a return visit, my cousin Nicole Forgeron wrote:

> *Hi Kathy! You're looking great! This will take time. Make sure you cooperate with everyone even though you may not think they know what they're doing. In a couple of weeks, you'll be out of here if you keep pushing yourself. We know that of all people, you can do it...but you really must be tough now. You have survived in here*

this long so you can last a few more days. We all pray for you each night. Somebody up there is listening to us. We'll be seeing you soon, hang tough.

My last visitor book entry is dated June 11th, 1993. My relative and dear friend, David Isherwood wrote, *"It's just me, Dave. Checking up on you and everything looks great. You've come a long way baby! Keep up the good work. Thinking of you, always."* Re-reading this entry I have a vague image of Dave walking in to visit me with his two sons. Details are still blurry and may be part of my imagination. Sadly, Dave passed away in 2019. Thinking of them walking into my room, happy memories return of his kindness and friendship.

Therapy

From a medical perspective, I realized much later how fortunate I was to have an interdisciplinary team of angels who worked with me every day. Pharmacotherapy coordinated a drug cocktail that took prior conditions into consideration. Before the crash I suffered from asthma and chronic bronchitis that were exasperated from injuries, so treatment was augmented with Prednisone. The complexity of my injuries had to be carefully managed and modified as conditions surfaced or worsened. Physically I had numerous problems requiring pain medication. Among the many internal bodily injuries resulting from the crash, my kidney and pancreas were bruised requiring monitoring.

During week 14, I was dealing with pneumonia, so I was given antibiotics. I had laser surgery to remove scar tissue from laryngeal edema in my throat (a complication of intubation and trauma to the larynx). Stress contributed to developing post-traumatic diabetes. My mental health issues were referred to a psychiatrist who diagnosed me with severe depression requiring additional drugs that would quell the symptoms but did not eliminate the underlying problems. Sometimes it appeared to be a matter of trial and error to get the right combination. There were times when my team of therapists raised concerns to my mother about my drug therapy because I was so out of it that I was unable to learn a thing.

Between my visitor and memory notebooks, there are not enough pages in this memoir to quote all the attempts made to improve the number one stumbling block to recovery, which was my negative attitude and perspective. Learning how to discern what is considered 'non-acceptable behaviour' so I could regulate my actions was critical, but it would take a very long time. Envisioning a better future was impossible as my perception was distorted.

I have memories of waking in the morning before my feet had even touched the floor being filled with dread as I became aware of my current situation. My mind and emotions created uncomfortable physical sensations that rushed from my gut filling me with anxiety. As I was getting ready for therapy, I worried about being able to follow instructions properly. I desperately wanted to get better, but when I heard a misstep being corrected, my senses picked up reprimand and criticism. My mother remembers a time when I was instructed to place coloured clothespins on a line in sequential order. I had to be shown the right sequence of patterning because I could not understand instructions or remember what was said moments before. My attention span was erratic, disrupting my willingness to continue.

Convincing myself that there is no shame in re-learning something when there is learning that needs to be done was not going to be easy. My mother believed my overall negativity stemmed from deep anxiety, and she compassionately tried to calm my fears. She would often say, *"I know you can't help it, but you have to try."* Being able to identify and name my fears remained elusive. Deep inside me, I knew all about positive psychology as I had my own repertoire of strategies and clichés to encourage my students to rise above adversity only months ago. However, my long-term memory that contained resilient tendencies was inaccessible for I was overwhelmed, simply grappling with what it took to get through every minute of the day.

Personal Goals

Anger was my predominant emotion and I needed to *'change the channel'*. I clung to the notion that I was a professional and despised these new feelings of being viewed simple-minded. It seemed that I was always being asked to monitor the negative side of my mind. I was expected to make a conscious effort to hush my dreadful feelings and picture a different kind of day than I was imagining. To tone down my anger, I was asked to consider the feelings of others and concentrate on *'positive and socially acceptable' comments."* I also had to focus on being cooperative and do my best to rebuild mental cognitive functions by following directions (memory, attention, language, etc.). One day during week 10, I wrote down three goals: 1) I talked with Shirley about my attitude with the nurses. She said I hurt their feelings. I know I need to change my attitude 2) I worked on red and yellow blocks 3) I worked on clothespins. I really hated doing these tasks as I was 35 years old being treated like I was in junior kindergarten.

It was a terrible struggle to believe that I could eventually get better if I only had the motivation to do so. My Mom has said many times that there were many days I refused to get dressed and start my day. I needed to channel my anger into something productive, so I had a good reason to get out of bed. My speech therapist repeatedly encouraged me to quietly say affirmations such as *"Be kind to myself"* to disrupt the negative pathways that were becoming entrenched in my brain.

The day I realized that becoming mobile was critical to get out of 'prison', I set a bigger goal. In my memory book I printed, *"Say I can, and I will."* I wanted to rebuild the strength in my arms and muscles so I could learn how to move by myself in a wheelchair. I also saw the value of working hard to improve my short-term memory and tried different strategies. For the most part I continued to record activities and appointments in my memory notebook without any other details. One day it became important to remember the names of my visitors, so I started writing their names while they were still there. By week 11, I printed the names of 16 visitors along with a few words on how we spent our time together. This was slow but sure progress.

Re-learning how to dress myself was another important goal. An early memory during my time in the hospital is when the occupational therapist 'taught' me how to put my socks and shoes on. I had to use adaptive aids that were hard to manipulate, and I became so frustrated that I threw my shoes against the wall. I hated depending on others to do something that used to be so simple. When I had to relearn how to put my bra on, I had to calm myself down first. I was left alone to practice using a shirt, putting it on my lap and doing up the buttons. I swore the entire time.

I knew my life was turned upside down. When I realized there were things I couldn't do, it made me feel incompetent and not 'Kathy the professional teacher' I used to be. The rehab staff repeatedly tried to explain that I had a 'head injury', and I didn't think there was anything wrong with my head nor did I have a full grasp of the implications. I felt better when I was reminded of good things I did. Week 12, a teacher at my school came to visit and uplifted my spirits:

> *Mrs. Levesque told me I taught her children religion...they said I was a good teacher. She made me feel it was okay to question the nurses about my medication ...Yes, I have a brain injury and it is getting better. I'm writing on my lap. That is why it is so messy.*

This was progress! The old Kathy deep inside of me was being affirmed, trust issues were being revealed, and I was even conscientious about my writing. I was beginning to acknowledge that I had a 'brain injury', mostly because I was repeating the explanation I was given every time I asked. Subsequent entries indicate that I did not really understand what a brain or head injury meant. I could see the physical injuries to my body but in my mind, there was nothing wrong with my brain.

Living in a Fog

Neuroscience is a promising new frontier offering hope that our thoughts can change the structure and function of our brains over time. The brain has the remarkable ability to adapt, grow, change, and learn. This is called remodeling (Bennett, 2022). My memory notebook helped me appreciate that despite living in a fog of confusion my brain was beginning to heal itself. At week 9 I was barely able to print. By week 13, I reached a milestone, writing in shaky large script. I began the entry by acknowledging my feelings, *"I am very angry at the person who hit my car and me ...He should be arrested and made to stay there as long as I am in the hospital ...I guess I have to pray for him and myself."* I still remember a visit by Father Roche who tried to reframe my thinking by saying the driver did not wake up that morning with the intention to hit my car. I was unable to grasp the rationale behind his thinking. Forgiving was just a word because I did not comprehend what it meant or how to deal with my anger.

Everything was confusing but I knew I had to stop depending on a wheelchair and learn how to walk again. I figured that once I learned how to do that, I could go back home. I desperately wanted to go back to the life I had before, including teaching school. But once I started realizing that I was now the student and the medical staff were the teachers, despair descended on me as I didn't know who 'Kathy' was anymore. Depression was affecting my thinking, mainly caused by confusing feelings of inadequacy. My identity was totally lost, and my spirit was broken. Sadness was overwhelming. I felt strangely isolated and misunderstood worsening the anger I felt. A new reality seeped into my consciousness dragging me further down into a deep depression.

Thoughts of being unable to escape and get the hell out of what had become a prison were always on my mind. Sister Emma was among those who understood. In all her visits there is one day that I will always remember. She found me crying and asked me to list the good things in my life. The entry is dated June 4th, fifteen weeks after the crash. I was able to write down 25 items, such as owning my home, appliances, and a lawnmower along with things I was able to do, such as being a teacher and able to drive for 16 years. Sr. Emma went on to add 20 more items that captured inner resilience. She noted my current progress such as being able to dress myself, brush my teeth and rebuild the strength in my arms so I could begin using a walker. She also noted I was thoughtful, appreciative and a fighter who bounced back from the hard times in my life. Sr. Emma was a pillar of spiritual strength in my healing journey providing a glimmer of hope. However, it was confusing to reconcile my confused distorted perceptions with her strong belief that I had the ability to get better. Without her unconditional love and friendship, I would undoubtedly have ended up on the psychiatric ward due to my depression, lack of control, and anger issues.

Acceptance is Elusive

I wanted to believe in the progress I was making that Sr. Emma mentioned, but impatience was getting to me. I was also irrational. Nighttime continued to bring out a full display of my obstinate tendencies. One night, I was determined to escape and get the hell out of there, but I needed to get to the wheelchair that was in the hallway next to the door of my room. I figured out how to use my good arm to unlatch the side of my bed where my good leg was, then take three steps to only fall flat on my face sending my glasses across the room. The nurses came running after hearing me swear and the commotion I caused. They put me back into bed with a few words of their own. The next night when I couldn't sleep, I was strapped into my wheelchair and sat at the nurses' station so they could keep an eye on me. To keep me busy they gave me a magazine, but I threw it right back at them. I was more than a handful and had to stay there until the midnight shift came on.

Another minor shift in my thinking appeared during week 15 when I began operating the wheelchair on my own. At this early stage of my recovery, I held firmly to the belief that one day I would return to my classroom as a teacher. I also saw myself being able to drive again. These were dreams and many medical professionals told my parents I was delusional. I could see that my broken body was beginning to heal giving me hope.

The day arrived when I was able to leave the hospital on a day trip in my wheelchair to the mall. I spotted a t-shirt that said, *'I love my attitude problem'* and my mother reluctantly bought it for me. When I heard the nurses say I had an 'attitude' problem, I defiantly put the shirt on and wheeled myself out to the nurses' desk so they could see it. My passive aggressive behaviour was displayed in full view. In my mind I didn't have a problem – they did!

Finding Purpose

Boredom was debilitating as the days dragged on in the hospital. A thoughtful and compassionate nurse saw an opportunity to keep me busy. She took me to a stock room and asked me to inventory face cloths, bath, and hand towels. When I got tired, she put me to bed. Counting became a daily 'job' for me after breakfast and dinner. My 'responsibilities' progressed to 'folding'. As the cart returned from the laundry, I was called over the P.A. to let me know the towels had arrived. Sometimes the nurses would even send me to the cafeteria to get drinks. I had a tray on my wheelchair and drove off with my list returning with the drinks and change. The responsibility triggered feelings of being important. I had a sense of purpose, as simple as it was, and in my delusion, I felt I was part of the staff. More importantly, anger settled down and my attitude improved, ever so slightly.

Self-awareness was slow to arrive through the confusing fog I was living. It was five months before I fully understood that I was severely injured due to a car crash. One day I was counting ceiling tiles as I was lying in bed. Interrupting my train of thought was a recurring message: "*You are just going to have to get used to spending the rest of your life relying on that wheelchair.*" I now had hope that things could change. As impossible as it seemed at the time, I simply did not want to be defeated by accepting this fate. Deep down my anger began fueling another thought. In my mind I began saying a different affirmation, repeating over and over, "*Just watch me!*"

The Past Resurfaces

During week 17, my therapist asked me to use my imagination and plan a trip. Daydreaming a different positive reality was a relief to the rumination of despair I found myself in. I spent hours planning an itinerary as an escape from the prison I was trapped in. I decided to use a travel agency so I could go to Florida's Epcot Centre and Disney World and stay in a hotel. I had relatives there so I included a visit with them where I would cook a scrumptious meal with all the fixings and ice cream for dessert. Visualizing revealed that my planning skills and ability to organize were beginning to surface and I could apply them to a different scenario even if it was make-believe. This was a healing problem-solving experience, revealing a part of brain plasticity at work. But there is not one word mentioned in this episode that I wrote in my memory book about positive emotions or how I would feel if I could get there. I continued to experience the *'blunt or flattened affect'.* This symptom of frontal lobe brain injury and the subsequent depression causes restrained or diminished emotional responses in certain situations.

Week 18 was full of activity. The time had come when I was facing my brain and physical limitations, realizing it was up to me to rebuild my health and emotional well-being. I was also making progress in physiotherapy by pushing myself. In a 1 ½ hour session, I worked foot pedals on a standing bike and then walked between the bars without a cane or walker: *"I walked depending on my feet and my brain. It was hard at first, but I made it work and did a good job. I didn't end up with a sore knee or leg."* Once when I had trouble sleeping a kind orderly brought me into the hall and stood beside me as I walked holding onto the rail. When I had to let go to move between rooms, he reassured me that he was right there to make sure I wouldn't fall. His confidence helped me believe that one day I would be able to walk without assistance.

At times I became a conniver to overcome my limitations. I was trying to adapt mostly because it was the only way I knew how to get what I wanted. I remember showing a nurse how I could walk down the hallway without help so she could see how happy this made me feel. Really, I was just hoping she would let me take a shower. It was very upsetting that they would not let me take one by myself. If I needed a bath, I had to have staff with me. In my mind I was robbed of my dignity, trapped in a prison and the guards were nurses. I was not realizing they were following protocols designed for my own safety. It was another example of deep feelings of shame and embarrassment clouding my perception as their hands moved across my body. All I wanted was to be left alone to take a shower. One day I was so frustrated I used the tap from the sink to drench myself yelling at the nurses to stay out saying, *"I am taking a bath."* Everyone was living the nightmare of my frustration.

Day Trips Begin

Taking responsibility for my erratic rude behaviour began to surface during week 20. I was very excited when a plan was being made for a trip to my parents' home, *"I am really hoping that I can act the right way and behave properly. When I first came here to the hospital, I really didn't understand what was wrong with me."* I was becoming more confident using a walker or cane, so it became easier to travel. The visit was a success, especially helping with routine chores, *"It felt really good to be domesticated."* A degree of self-confidence was settling in as I was experiencing a slight shift into a level-headed acceptance of my life's circumstances.

Memory of an earlier trip to Banff, Alberta

Another escape into freedom was a trip back to my own house. I wrote that I was worried about not knowing what to expect and ended the entry by saying, "I *really didn't want to return to the hospital. It was great to be able to sit under a tree in my backyard."* Being in nature was always calming for me easing the stress and anxiety of day-to-day life. I found comfort revisiting many happy long-term memories, recalling my Dad taking the family for a car ride to explore local woodlots or going on boat rides to enjoy the day at Peche Island. Every year we visited my Mom's family who live in Nova Scotia surrounded by nature's beauty. Another special memory was a trip into the majestic mountains of Banff, Alberta. I often dwelled on the past, yearning to be free so I could once again connect with the Creator's breath-taking beauty. Thinking about peaceful memories briefly helped ease the tide of despair.

Over the next several weeks my memory book was filled with brief outlines of my daily routines including news about visitors and sessions with doctors and therapists. I also wrote about going to my uncle's wedding reception and that my friend Jeannie Albert came all the way from Montreal to spend time with me. Another highlight that week was attending our St. Anne's graduation. Two years before I started an 'Exceptional Kindness Award' in memory of my sister Myra and one of my students was being recognized for his compassion toward special needs students. In the lengthiest entry of my memory notebook, I seemed impatient about waiting to be picked up then shifted to trying to understand my changed circumstances:

> *The time from 1 p.m. to 4 p.m. was very long, it almost felt like one week. I think it's because I'm getting out of here and going somewhere else...Every time I talk about school, I feel as if a part of me is missing. It's probably because I spent so much time there and really gave school every moment I had.*

The entry went on listing my past involvement in the life of the school, including retreats, dances, football games, can drives, raising money for the poor and helping at the Special Olympics. I also organized and went on field trips to Cedar Point and Toronto. A deeper recognition of my past was surfacing as I was able to re-imagine events stored in my long-term memory. Taking the time to recall the kindness I extended to others helped me recognize inner resilient tendencies that I needed to draw on. But interestingly, once again, there is no mention of joy, happiness, or sadness. Sadly, there are still times when numbness takes hold and uplifting feelings remain elusive.

Relationships

I felt disconnected as some of my relationships were changing. As my compassionate friend Arlene Veitch explained, *"Sometimes people just don't know what the best thing to do when someone goes through a traumatic experience."* There is not much to say about my romantic interest, except he abandoned me while I was in the hospital without explanation. It would take a very long time to recover from the rejection. My focus turned to those who continued to show up in my life despite the difficulties I was facing. Details were important when I wrote about the short-day trips I was taking, outlining where I went, who was there, what we ate, or what we did.

One special trip was a return to the SNJM convent on Peter Street. Relationships with my religious community developed into forever friendships, and even though I never took my final vows I became an associate years later, *"I was a part of their family for eight years. I felt like a real star because everyone greeted me."* I believe their gift of acknowledgment helped me realize that 'who I really am' - the authentic part of me - made a difference in the lives of others. I was grateful for all their dedicated concern to visit and pray for me. Their steadfast love became spiritual nourishment in my healing journey.

Companions on the journey to become a Sister of the Holy Names of Jesus and Mary

I needed to find meaning in my life by recognizing the limitations I was facing and start building on my strengths. My speech therapist encouraged me to recall past acts of kindness and write about them. My Dad painted my sheds, and in gratitude I bought him a card. I acknowledged that my brother Philip bought me a coke and my sister Pauline did my laundry. I gave Linda Shearon a birthday card and wished her a happy day. These are all little gestures that I began to realize are important. I also wrote about a positive conversation I had with my respirology doctor. I viewed him as being curt, uncaring, and unsympathetic having argued with him about my medication weeks before. Contrary to what I perceived as being misunderstood, he commented on how good I was doing with my weight. It wasn't planned or intentional but losing weight helped ease my breathing, asthma, and post traumatic diabetes.

My defensive critical judgement was wavering: *"Today I felt like we had a common respect for one another."* All my life, weight management has been a struggle and the source of some of my unhappiest memories. When I arrived in the hospital, I weighed more than 200 pounds, and I am only 5 feet tall. The doctor's affirmation was a celebration of sorts, in line with my lifelong efforts to lose weight. A seed had been planted to get serious about getting my weight under control.

Hospital Stay Draws to a Close

After six months in the hospital the time to consider alternate arrangements was approaching and my parents fought hard to ensure I could get support to stay in my own house. A transition to overnight stays started taking place and limitations surfaced with the usual negative emotions of frustration:

> *Yesterday I fell in the living room. I felt really bad about it and started to cry. I felt really angry with the guy who hit me because now I don't really have balance... Tonight I felt really upset about the fact that I forgot how to tune and play my guitar. I have been playing it for about 13 years and I can't believe how I forgot.*

Deep feelings of loss were finally being acknowledged and expressed privately in my memory book. I was beginning to recognize the reality of physical, emotional, and mental difficulties before me. Whether I was mentally prepared for the next phase of my recovery or not, the psychologist at the hospital informed us that the medical team was recommending that I be discharged as an outpatient with the provision that my physiotherapy, speech

Memory of playing my guitar

and occupational sessions continue. I needed continued support to strengthen my body, improve my short-term memory, correct my speech problems, and in general adjust to the physical surroundings at my home. With considerable help being provided, I was hoping that I could focus on working toward other goals such as using a computer, playing my guitar, and becoming fully independent.

Half a year after the crash I expressed concerns that the next phase of my healing journey would be an uphill climb living at home. I was grateful that another compassionate psychologist would be included in my healing circle of care for I was still in the deep grips of depression. Every aspect of my life had been disrupted and I still did not realize the turmoil I was causing to everyone in some way or another:

> *Today is Sunday and because of my tough day yesterday I didn't feel good enough to go to church. I felt down, depressed and very negative. My PSW had to put up with a lot of guff. She spent a whole hour talking with me about how far I have come since my car crash. She wrote down a list of my accomplishments this far. When she was going to throw the paper away, I said I wanted it.*

My personal support worker was patiently trying to help me recognize the progress I made. Resilient tendencies were returning, and I was being reminded to embrace healthy thoughts, keep things in perspective and work on having a hopeful outlook. On August 29th, 1993, I took her listing of milestones that chronicled my hospital journey and rewrote it in my memory book - most of which I have already mentioned. As I was being discharged, the nurses said if I needed to return, they would be there for me. I remember thinking, “That won’t ever happen if I had anything to say about it.”

Recovering from TBI is a personal mountainous journey with deep valleys and steep slopes to climb. I found the rate of improvement depends on developing an internal sense of self-awareness and strength needed to work through the different stages of healing. It was extremely disturbing that I could not understand the changes that were happening. I was leaving the hospital hopeful even with my angry, distorted perception of reality. On one level I wanted to be an active participant in the internal work of recovery but ‘how’ to go about it was not yet within my grasp.

Nurse Linda Proctor graciously provided a reflection during my stay in the rehab hospital. She was among those truly ‘present’ with their gifts of encouragement and spiritual nourishment during my most cantankerous moments. Prayers for forgiveness were whispered in the quiet of the night long after I left. Today I can truly appreciate the compassionate understanding and care given to me by front line nurses. Linda’s medical perspective illustrates the roller coaster of highs and lows attributed to brain injury, weaving my emotional behaviour into intrinsic and extrinsic motivational qualities underlying my recovery and stay in rehab:

> *Some miracles do happen every day. As an RPN, (Registered Practical Nurse) working in the Inpatient Rehab Unit, we saw many joyous moments, and some truly sad ones as we worked with quadriplegics, paraplegics, amputees, stroke survivors, and brain injury patients. All have their challenges, but to me, the brain injury was indeed the most challenging mainly because every brain injury patient reacts differently to their diagnosis.*
>
> *Brain injuries can provoke a whole host of emotions that normally the person would not exhibit. Anger, rage, tempers, some physical, some just verbal. Kathy had a definite stubborn streak, and some days had to be cared for with kid gloves. She also had a laugh that could wipe away all the drama and make yourself laugh.*

Most days she attended her physio and occupational therapy classes. Her Mom, thankfully, had a way with Kathy, able to calm her down so she would participate in activities she preferred to avoid. Watching Kathy progress from a wheelchair to a walker, to a cane was a great sign. She was doing her job, and we were doing ours.

I was often assigned to her care, but she certainly could test my patience at times. One incident stands out from all the rest, that Kathy and I still laugh about. After a morning of therapy, and after her lunch, I settled her in for her nap so I could catch up on my paperwork. She could see me from her room and kept calling for me to come back. She wasn't having any excuses or the line "I'll be there in a minute!" Next thing I knew, my Head Nurse was holding the phone laughing. Apparently, Miss Kathy called 911 from her room phone to report me to the Windsor police!!! After a brief discussion with the police, we all had a good laugh...and Kathy promised never to do it again.

Kathy's life has been a challenge for her and her family since the accident, but she has handled it with grace and determination. I have stayed connected with her throughout these past 29 years and we exchange our life's stories from time to time. Life, as it is with everyone, has its ups and downs, but Kathy has blossomed. Knowing Kathy has brought a joy to my life.

Part III

Navigating the Storm

Fate whispers to the warrior, 'You cannot withstand the storm.'
The warrior whispers back, 'I am the storm.'
Author Unknown

Joy was a welcomed emotion when I was greeted by a house full of visitors welcoming me home. A new journey awaited as I left the confines of the rehabilitation hospital to continue 24-hour nursing and medical care. My parents had power of attorney and secured the help of my lawyer Greg Monforton, who successfully argued with insurance companies to make the transition as an outpatient financially possible. An interdisciplinary medical team was organized to sustain the gains made in my rehabilitation program and I was excited for the change of routine: *"I am finally finished with my occupational, physio and speech therapies at the hospital. One-hour weekly treatments will continue as an out-patient."*

The freedom I yearned for had begun and a clear memory capturing the feeling was when I took my very first shower in my own bathroom. My bodily senses became alert as I sat on a stool in the tub by myself. I enjoyed the privacy and sensation of warm water washing away all the weariness, leaving me feeling peaceful and serene. I felt refreshed, smelling good all over from the Caprina Fresh Goat's Milk Soap given to me in a gift basket. Even today I still use it and when I lay quietly in bed, the smell stirs good feelings of being renewed.

Freedom though was fleeting and the adjustment to home health care was not easy. for eight weeks I had 24-hour nursing care. Personal support workers and their supervisors arrived to cook, clean, and basically tell me when to wake up, dress, eat, bathe and finally when to go to bed. Being dependent on so many strangers who came into my home to take care of my needs made me feel like I was being babysat. It was not easy to accept, especially in the early days when privacy was still not a possibility, even to close my bedroom door to get dressed.

Major hurdles lay ahead in my new life's circumstances and the road to recovery was still long and winding. Events causing adversity are inevitable throughout everyone's life, and the crash made me realize that I was not an exception. Being sent home from the hospital marked the beginning of a different adaptive process requiring a major adjustment in expectations. It became critical that I take the next step of acknowledging my newly acquired limitations, some that were obvious and others that remained hidden for a very long time. I needed help in identifying stressors so I could learn how to cope with the chaotic upheavals and the inevitable conflicts of life, that before would have rolled off my back.

Psychological Therapy

There were so many reminders that I was living in a chaotic storm of upheaval. My entire life had been turned upside down. I went from being a professional life skills teacher to relearning basic skills so I could rebuild every single part of myself. Of concern to my healing circle of care were the continuing episodes of frustration that spilled into intense anger, as quickly as flipping a switch. Thankfully, during my last month in the hospital, psychological therapy began. That doctor really knew how to handle me when I said something inappropriate, cruel, or insulting. She would abruptly say, *"I have heard enough!"* I had no alternative but to pause, which helped me recognize that sometimes I really did not have a point to make and I was just venting. I didn't realize how much I was focused on getting my own way. I was unable to consider her needs or feelings as a person. In some cases, self-centredness is a brain injury tendency that becomes a destructive form of thinking. It would be much later before I could identify the different changes in my personality and recognize how my behaviour was diminishing the person I wanted to be.

When I went home another compassionate psychologist took up my case. I worked with Dr. Carol Franklyn for the next six years from August 3rd, 1993, to August 11th, 1999. At first, I continued to use my memory notebook and then started journaling. When I left her care she gave me a copy of her case notes, an invaluable gift in piecing together this time in my life. Years later research helped me make sense of those intense sessions and deepened my understanding of TBI beyond personal experience.

During my first visit to her office, I remember looking straight into her eyes and felt a calm reassurance that she would be there every step of the way. Her respectful approach fostered feelings of dignity and self-worth. Being able to agree or disagree with her made it easier to hear what she was saying:

> *I met my new psychologist, and she is the first person who explained to me about my head injury. I felt like she treated me as an educated person who could understand what happened to me. She will see me once a week. She said she will work with me on the grieving process over my accident and changes in my body so I can understand what happened to me.*

Psychology was my minor specialty in university, yet I was confused what she meant by 'the grieving process.' I realized people treated me differently and I had deep resentment when I felt someone was talking down to me or treating me like a child. My perspective was skewed, and I was still unable to acknowledge the drastic changes in my personality or completely understand what had happened to my body. Anger was always bubbling below the surface. I could not feel deep sorrow caused by loss or view the crash as a chance misfortune encountered on that fateful Ash Wednesday morning.

My psychologist became a person I could trust with my deepest vulnerabilities and inner truths. I can still see myself sitting in her office. Emotions return as I revisit memories of the underlying issues that continue to impact my mental, physical, emotional, and spiritual well-being. We were peeling back the onion skin and the first layer was the degree of resistance to accept the effects of my injuries. Gently but firmly, she helped me adjust my expectations so I could deal with day-to-day turmoil. We tackled an array of fears causing severe anxiety and inappropriate behaviour by reframing the effects of stressful situations. I learned how to adapt as a traumatic brain injured survivor, which was critical to improving my mental health.

We often revisited positive interactions from my past life, which helped me understand that as a teacher I had earned the respect of my colleagues because of the compassionate way I treated others. To change my erratic behaviour, we celebrated small steps of progress. Even though I still desperately wanted the old Kathy back, I started to recognize that I had to let go of the old Kathy so a renewed Kathy could be born. I just had to figure out how to do this with her help.

Therapeutic and Surgical Care

I traveled to the hospital as an out-patient for therapy. Becoming self-aware of my strengths was a slow process to bounce back from my limitations. Trusting those who oversaw my 'curative' program was a major struggle. For nine months I took a cab three days a week to see my speech language, occupational, and physio therapists. The trips affected me mentally. I detested being dependent on strangers taking me back and forth to my appointments. Before I even arrived at my appointment, my mind was in a negative spiral: *"Every time I go back into the hospital, I think that somehow, they will entrap me back into the prison."*

The best part of the week was going to speech and language therapy. I was very comfortable with my therapist Elaine because she treated me like an adult instead of a child. We worked on improving my short-term memory and I felt like I was actively participating in the plan. She had many resources and learning strategies that were familiar to me: *"We had a lot of fun playing memory games with puzzles and numbers."* She used copies of the Readers Digest and other magazines to help me recall pictures with corresponding words. I also remember watching comedies including Willy Wonka's Chocolate Factory, a favourite of mine. We talked about funny parts helping to rebuild my recall ability and that lifted my spirits.

The occupational therapy program was especially frustrating because it reminded me of the self-care and daily living activities that I taught in my life skills program. Realizing I was the 'disabled student' and not the 'teacher' was beyond disheartening. I really hated being there and I could not understand why I was being put through 'their program'. In my mind, I was the one who should be in charge because I was an accomplished educator who had developed countless individualized programs for my students. I felt the therapist's assessment of my programming needs was just part of her imagination. In my mind I continued to think there was nothing wrong with my brain. I was miserable and took my bitterness out on the therapist. Each time I had an explosive episode, my mother or Dr Franklyn would tell me I needed to apologize, which I reluctantly did. It was a trade-off for I was learning that being compliant would help me get my way for other things.

In physiotherapy I was making progress using a walker but often depended on a wheelchair: *"I like physiotherapy because it is helping me re-learn how to walk. I know that my knee and broken tibia bone are the problem. Not my brain."* It was interesting that I could not see a connection between my broken bones and my damaged brain. I had to do the work to regain my strength and mind/muscle connection by balancing myself then move between the parallel bars. It was not easy. I was so nervous not wanting to release my hands from the security of the crossbars. My therapist tried many different strategies to help me relearn how to walk independently but my self-confidence was weakened. When I went home, I often cried. It was very difficult to get past the physical pain and what seemed to be never-ending futility.

I was also dealing with negative feelings due to an inability to perform simple physical activities that prior to the crash were very easy. Eleven months after the crash I needed to have surgery on my knee and right tibia to remove the plate and screws (January 26th, 1994). Returning to the hospital for an operation once again filled me with anticipatory anxiety and my psychologist helped to calm the imagined fears. When I returned home three weeks after my surgery, I was able to bring the plate, screws and pins that were removed.

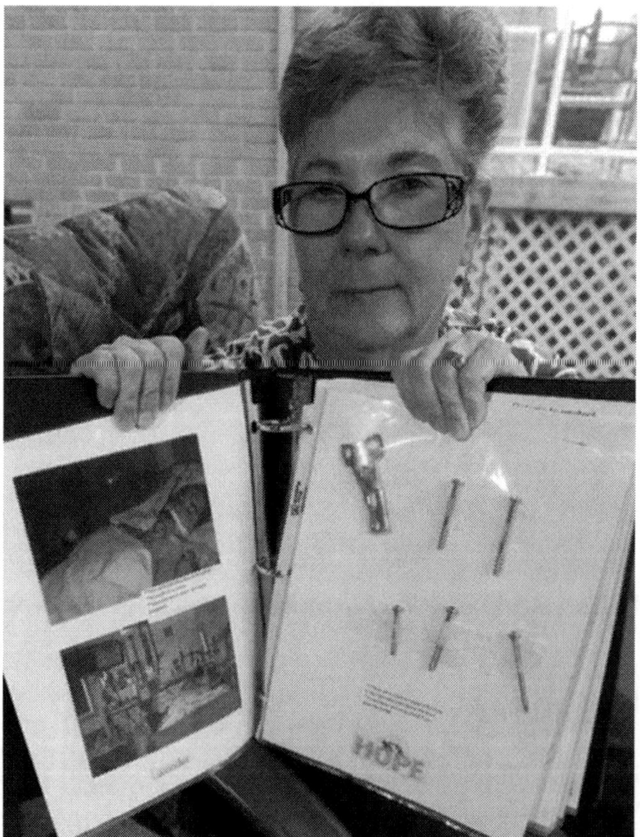

Memories of my time in the hospital from my scrapbook

Dr. Franklyn expressed surprise that my spirits were *'somewhat lifted'* and predicted that I would be able to move further along in physiotherapy. My goal was walking independently but I needed to regain confidence so I could progress from a walker to a cane and then to walking sticks. I still use these to help me stay steady when I walk in the woods behind my house.

Moving Forward with Home Care

Occupational therapists and personal support workers came into my home to help me learn how to organize myself. I had to relearn simple tasks so I could do my own grocery shopping, cooking, and laundry. Most importantly I wanted to take care of my personal hygiene in the shower. Acceptance of my new reality continued to be a gradual process mostly because I was full of resentment that my world had been turned upside down. Being dependent on others in my own home was particularly stressful. Dr. Franklyn tried to help me learn how to cope with day-to-day situations by identifying normal 'environmental stressors' that were made much worse by the damage to my brain. Each week she helped me reframe my skewed perception to understand the complexity of my problems. She helped me see there were many ways to interpret a situation. Her delicate method of questioning my misgivings uncovered a conviction that everyone was out to harm me instead of simply doing their job with good intention. That point of view took a long time to shift. Mistrust created delusions of persecution impacting my confidence and self-esteem. Dr. Franklyn encouraged me to release my emotional suffering through creative means and suggested that I write poetry. When I was home alone, I turned to my journal and began expressing my feelings:

Powerless, Growth, Pain

I am powerless
MY LIFE IS UNMANAGEABLE
I can no longer take control of all the events in my life
I feel like a rubber band being stretched and bounced
From crisis to crisis
ANGER
RESENTMENT
BLAMING
NEGATIVITY
RESISTANCE
These stop me from walking the path to recovery

A Troubling Journey into Self Discovery

I was willing to share my poetry and after listening, Dr. Franklyn tried to help me see a different reality of gifts and blessings. Patiently, she tried to illustrate how each person in my life was dedicated in their own way to help me succeed. My mother also provided a calming presence at each of the countless medical and therapy appointments, but I was stuck in a negative mindset and unable to shift my point of view. My words and actions did not make it easy for everyone around me.

By May 1994 my trips to the hospital as an out-patient came to an end. Home care continued and with the help from Dr. Franklyn I was navigating the obstacles of adjusting to the next phase in recovery. There are many factors that medical professionals need to consider in designing treatment plans. Everyone has unique personality traits that make us who we are. Meetings were held with my parents and other members of my family to develop a pre-crash and post-crash profile. The exercise was intended to better understand how to resolve the problems that developed. My cousin Anne Boudreau described some of my qualities:

> *We have always been emotionally connected, so she has been like a sister to me. Growing up I always appreciated her humour, sensitivity, kindness, interest in God, love of our family, and her way of singing "It's raining it's pouring." Our entire family knew she was struggling to get better, and I had faith that she was strong willed enough to find her way back.*

From a medical perspective I was under a microscope as professionals considered my personality type, pre-injury abilities, and degree of brain damage at a given point in time. Numerous reports were prepared providing opinions about my condition. Two neuropsychologists agreed that there was evidence that I was experiencing gradual neurologic improvement. Findings reported a shift from a diffuse axonal brain injury causing severe premorbid functionality to moderate with ongoing deficits:

> *She is unfortunately left with significant neurocognitive dysfunction predominantly related to bilateral frontal lobe compromise ...Given the time lapsed, it is most likely that these neurocognitive deficits will be permanent in nature...these deficits indicates that she is unlikely to return to competitive employment.*

I was unable to comprehend the extent of my 'neurocognitive' limitations and the words 'deficits' will most likely be 'permanent in nature' did not make sense. For several years, Dr. Franklyn noted that I had limited awareness or insight into the bi-frontal lobe changes affecting my personality and behaviour. Our conversations revealed defensive tendencies that were exasperated by blaming others and being resentful, argumentative, aggressive, and irrational. In general, I was out of touch with reality.

We spent considerable time unravelling my self-righteous perceptions when she would ask, *"Would you have reacted like this before your crash?"* Of course, I would say *"no,"* which opened the door to reconsider my thinking. When she asked me to "think about where you were before the crash", I could talk about traits that served me well that now had drawbacks. Patience was never one of my best virtues as noted by my family. My teaching colleagues also knew that when I thought something needed to be done, I wanted it done as soon as possible. Arlene Veitch, a teaching colleague also described the old 'Kathy' that I desperately wanted back:

> *When I first met you Kathy, I met this vibrant, fun-loving, lively, happy person. I loved spending time with you. I would often go into your classroom because I always came out uplifted. I also saw how resilient you were when you had a very sad occurrence in your life --- when your sister Myra died so quickly after being diagnosed with a deadly blood disease. You just stepped right in and helped raise her children. I saw that side of you, where you could do anything that needed to be done.*

I could envision changes for improvement to the quality of life for my students and I was fearless in presenting my ideas to the principal. He good-naturedly shook his head at my persistence when I wanted an update about my request. Impatience was exasperated by the effects of traumatic brain injury, and my quick tempered, impulsive, irritable comments made interactions difficult. So, I got on the nerves of my family and many medical professionals, just another psychosocial implication from my brain impairment.

Explaining why safety protocols were in place, one of my personal support workers often reminded me to simply accept my 'limitations' as part of my 'brain injury'. Her way of dealing with my resistance was extremely upsetting. After I complained numerous times, she was removed from my care. This intensified my goal to have all home assistance removed. I saw their presence as an invasion of my privacy, and not taking care of a need to keep me safe. I desperately wanted to retake a sense of control over my life. The truth was, there were times when I would scheme by quietly slipping out of the house in the dark of night and use my walker to go to the bank, putting myself at risk. Dr, Franklyn had a daunting task to help me reframe my perspective so I could strengthen the positive pathways in my brain and avoid excessive defense reactions.

Professional Reviews

Professionals conducted numerous interviews that built on previous reports to provide an opinion of my progress. Sixteen months after the crash my insurance company requested a third neuropsychological report to determine my ability to function independently in the world and possible career options. The summary below briefly highlights the doctor's observations and recommendations:

Physical complaints: Surgery removed plate, pins, and screws in right tibia bone

Fatigue: Still evident - 1 ½ hour nap taken in afternoon - major disruptive sleep patterns at night

Eating habits: Improving, difficulty swallowing food due to scar tissue from intubation continues - on a weight watcher program to lose weight - continuing goal established during hospital stay.

Retrograde amnesia: Inability to recall remains problematic – extent is approximately 24 hours.

Memory deficits: Psychologist is helping to compensate forgetfulness by using numerous memory enhancement and compensation techniques

- Large daybook used to note what is expected each hour of the day replacing the memory book used in the hospital – columns display a 'to do' list, important activities and appointments
- People are asked to call before meetings as a reminder
- Post it notes used to inform what was inside each cupboard and drawer

Attention: Difficulty in concentrating

- Learning strategies such as positioning body improve focus and ability to hear what is said
- Background noise unbearable at times so carries ear plugs

Concept formation and problem solving: Confusion evident

- Problems with concentration, sustained attention, issues with direction so tries to:
- Visualize landmarks
- Counting steps – keeps a notepad and pencil in purse to write down starting point to be able to retrace steps
- Put things away in the same place

Word finding fluency: No difficulties

Reading and writing: Ability to express herself using poetry and daybook

Family relations: Applying adaptive strategies and coping techniques when issues surface

Social life: Good network of friends hampered by problems in travelling to see people

Personality functioning, anger, mood: Occasional outbursts of anger from feelings of inability to perform activities that prior to the accident were easy to carry out:

- quite resentful not being able to work

- otherwise appears quite normal and adaptive

Vocation (Work): Personal goal is a return to teaching but need for more assessments to determine future work and training programs as vocational alternatives

Driving: Kathy's personal goal is to resume as soon as possible but cannot recommend at this time

Counselling: Continue working with psychologist to help her impulse control as well as her frustration tolerance; help Kathy deal with issues of loss that may arise as a result of her reported accident (e.g., career, independence, etc.); help her cope with the frustration of failures that are likely to occur

Occupational Therapy: Continue working with occupational therapist to provide organization in her daily routine and ensure safety during daily activities such as cooking ...training should be structured such that she is afforded success to maintain and improve feelings of self-esteem.

When I first received a copy of the report and discussed it with Dr. Franklyn, I ranted and raved. Here I was dealing with another doctor's opinion about my 'brain injury stupidity' and it was filled with bu** sh**. Emotionally, I continued to swear as my 'go to' way of expressing overwhelming feelings of loss for the parts of my life that were taken away from me. Especially disturbing was not being able to drive or return to my teaching position. Dr. Franklyn became my saving grace as she patiently and calmly helped me reframe my perspective so I could recognize that the report had positive comments as well including continued therapeutic and psychological support. After my negative energy calmed down, it became apparent that it was useless to think my situation would change back to what it once was. The logic did not change future emotional outbursts and the ruminating brain loop I was stuck on. Thoughts of not being viewed as 'intelligent' is a self-esteem problem that still lingers creating doubt that impacts my self-confidence.

There was no way around it. Those who cared for me were trying to help me navigate a new reality. Each day I was relearning coping skills to reach a personal goal of being self-reliant and functionally independent. But I had to find a way to lift myself out of the deep well of physical, mental, and emotional despair so I could become responsible for my own self-care. An important step was acknowledging my own resistance. I wanted to get unstuck but first I needed to identify and accept what I could not change or control. A significant challenge was accepting the findings and recommendations made in official reports. I was thinking that words are easily said but I had lingering doubts that no one could really understand what was going on inside of me.

Navigating a New Personality

From the very beginning of our sessions, Dr. Franklyn helped me identify triggers so I would become more self-aware and better able to manage my behaviour (October 6, 1993). So much was out of my control causing relentless feelings of anger, frustration and sadness that persisted for years, interfering with my psychosocial interactions. At times my uninhibited wrath would be stirred up whenever someone reminded me of something I simply forgot, a casualty of memory loss. I often interpreted comments as criticism and reacted without thinking. I would become frustrated, often spraying blame by blurting out, *"How come I wasn't told about that?"* Interestingly, I have been told that the charming part of my personality could emerge moments after an explosion with absolutely no memory on my part. Projecting blame is typical for a TBI victim, and I was continuing to exhibit rapid changeability in the way I expressed my emotions.

In our discussions relationship issues became a priority that needed to be urgently addressed. Expressions of aggression is a common debilitating consequence of TBI. Dr. Franklyn noted that my anger appeared to be intense and deep rooted, but the underlying cause was "not immediately clear." A major need to be addressed from the past was reconciling the death of my sister with events that followed. Just over two years before the crash, my sister Myra died at 26 years old from the blood disorder, thrombocytopenia. I was single and willingly became a caregiver for my nephews, helping my brother-in-law, Norm. I routinely stopped by, and I often prepared meals. Despite the heartache of losing my sister, I have precious memories of sharing their day-to-day life. I can still remember the day Matthew, at 3 years old, dressed himself and came down the stairs feeling so proud, even though his shirt was inside out and backwards. Another time was taking Adam to his first day at school. Joy and love for one another deepened as my entire family stepped in to help Norm and his sons.

After the crash I was very upset that I could no longer care for my two nephews that I loved dearly. My family dynamics had changed as I had to rely on significant support rather than being a caregiver. My loving tendencies vanished as feelings of intimacy and closeness were lost to numbness. Further complicating matters were moments when I insensitively blurted out exactly what was on my mind. I lacked empathy and had a short fuse, waiting impatiently for things to be done in my time, not theirs. I misunderstood intentions, thinking no one really cared about my needs and wants. Like others who suffer from TBI, the preoccupation with my own personal needs caused self-centredness. These are all characteristics that will test the strongest of family relationships.

Everyone in my family was adjusting to my 'new personality'. Not only did I fly off the handle but the reactions from family members could get very intense as well. Their tolerance was weakening as they dealt with my ongoing frustration. If a disagreement persisted, I needed Dr. Franklyn's help as an objective outsider to provide a different perspective. She recognized that communication issues are very sensitive with a patterned history in all families and ours was not an exception: *"Difficulties were reported in the communication department even before the crash took place"* (July 7, 1994). She brought us together several times for counselling to help ease the building frustration by explaining the consequences of brain injury. We each had our own concerns, which often overlapped. To reduce the escalating tensions, she suggested that we each pause before reacting. Recommendations to respond in a healthy manner included: i) ignore comments, ii) change the subject, iii) leave the scene, iv) consider the intention, and v) listen deeply and give the benefit of doubt to the speaker. These suggestions were helpful but in the heat of the moment it was difficult to implement especially for me. Overcoming the stress that harmed my family relationships became the most significant concern for all of us.

For six years Dr. Franklyn helped me develop coping strategies to improve my interactions. I was often reminded that people do not really understand the damage caused by brain injury. If I thought conflict was on the rise, and felt I was about to explode I needed to use the same simple strategies that the rest of my family was practicing. In addition, I needed to: i) begin deep breathing to help refocus, ii) repeat self-affirmations such as "It's not worth it!" iii) give myself permission to ignore and not respond. Dealing with the intense anger that caused me to lash out at my family took considerable time to automatically recall these simple choices.

Communication Problems

Being in stressful situations is part of day-to-day life, but reactions are exasperated with TBI. I started to become more consistent in dealing with mood changes by talking it out. Dr. Franklyn often asked me to consider an alternative way to respond empowering me to reconsider why I held onto my defiant and argumentative attitude. I was trying to redirect my anger and aggression and despite the strategies I was given, communication problems persisted. There were many times when other people did not understand my questions, opinions, or point of view leading to feelings of being defeated and extreme sadness.

The problems I developed by not recognizing the emotions of others and being unable to rationalize how my behaviour was offensive, slowed the pace of changing my negative tendencies. I needed to inhibit my impulsive remarks, especially to my mother who unconditionally loved me and never gave up believing that I would get better. She always acted out of unconditional love and did not deserve my abuse. She continually forgave me saying, *"I know this not you, but your brain injury coming out."* With little empathy, apologizing was not easy because I was convinced that I was not doing anything wrong. I now realize it took significant endurance, sensitive listening, faith, and considerable energy by those who believed that I would get better, to work with me one day at a time.

The importance of mindful thinking about potential consequences was a constant reminder throughout the years we worked together. In the second year of my recovery, I over-simplified my role in times of conflict because I really did not care. I also struggled with finding the right words and worried about being misunderstood. Sometimes there were frustrating moments when I had a 'brain freeze', stopping in mid-sentence and forgetting what I was talking about. Other times I grappled for the right words to communicate effectively. I was unable to recognize that the primary source of misunderstandings is caused by TBI communication problems. My cousin, Marlene Landry from Nova Scotia recognized that parts of the old Kathy were still present, however changed and filled with insecurities:

> *Brain injury can be mysterious to those who know the personality of the person. Before the tragic event, I saw Kathy in one light and then she found herself become a different person, but in some ways her personality remained the same. I listened to her from a distance*

> *over the phone. There was a sense of slowness in her speech. Her responses were well calculated, which I found interesting. It seemed like her brain needed additional time to process questions and consider what the right answer should be when she spoke. Her intelligence was still there in her answers; however, she seemed somewhat nervous as to whether the words she wanted to say were actually coming out of her mouth. She seemed worried whether I was able to hear the same message that she was trying to give.*

Fostering self-awareness of my actions became an integral component of our weekly discussions. Even though I tried to remember that other people did not really understand the consequences of brain injury, it would take time to return to the compassionate person that I was. A change in my reactions became noticeable when I began to take responsibility to think about what I could do to improve communication. Being able to compromise with others also became essential to re-build a sense of mutuality in my existing relationships as well as the new ones that were now entering my life.

Without doubt, I was receiving considerable support, which is critical in recovery. But accepting it gracefully was hampered by simmering anger that interfered with my ability to be genuinely grateful. I recognized that my Dad was always helping me around my house without being asked and one day I realized I had to make a specific effort to tell him how much I appreciated and loved him. After I gave my Dad a card, I mentioned it to Dr. Franklyn. She offered encouragement to reach out to others with small gestures that are mutually uplifting: "*Random acts of kindness could be used to rejuvenate her spirits when she is down, since it enhances her sense of worth*" *(January 11, 1995).*

Faith Remains Elusive

Despite the countless prayers and words of encouragement, I was struggling to find any meaning in all of what was going on. There were many times when I was left paralyzed and unable to navigate the situations I could not control. I still remember being overwhelmed by hopelessness and extreme feelings of frustration. Faith that somehow things will work out has always been at the Centre of my parents' beliefs. As Catholics my family believed in the power of compassionate love taught by Jesus, "I have come as light into the world, that whoever believes in me may not remain in darkness" (John 12:46). The darkness included a lack of empathy, and the numbness left me scared. My loving forever friendships with the Sisters of the Holy Names of Jesus and Mary remained steadfast in their faith and helped to bring a 'renewed Kathy' with my unique gifts back to my family and friends. I knew I was in their daily prayers but making sense of my misfortune troubled me deeply:

> *I met Kathy when she was a Sister of the Holy Names of Jesus and Mary. My memory recalls her vividly as a young woman. Life for Kathy at that time was a happy adventure. Each person she encountered had her full attention and her smiling eyes. I loved her stories about teaching students with special needs, how she enjoyed them and how she related to them told me that they knew they were loved by their teacher. The months after the crash I felt helpless and feared that I would never again hear her 'upbeat' voice and get one of her special genuine hugs. We prayed for her and as time went on, she was constantly struggling, climbing out of a deep, dark, confusing place. Sure, I saw her frustration during very difficult days. But during these times she moved through it and just showed her determination to reach clarity and full light. (Sister Helen Petrimoulx, SNJM)*

Sister Helen understood the depth of loneliness I felt being disconnected from my faith. I tried to cover up my despair and it took years to move through the field of thorns I found myself in. The dark feelings that accompanied extreme anger emerged from my mind because of the hand that 'fate' dealt me. Despite the rich faith tradition, I grew up in, I could not understand and asked repeatedly, *"Why me God?"* In my angry mind I hated God and felt justified in my feelings but at the same time felt guilty having these thoughts. My faith always helped me get through the most difficult times of my life, including the death of my younger sister Myra. I desperately wanted to believe that I would get better, but my day-to-day reality created doubt that healing was ever going to be possible:

Recovery

I came to believe that a Power greater than myself
could restore me to sanity.
God ...I knocked, I waited, I pleaded
Yet I did not open my heart to let you in.

God, this time of painful growth
has been very long and lonely.
In my weariness I feel unheard, I feel unwanted.
Yet in my pain I did not desire to ask for your help
I experienced disappointment.
I felt like my inner space
was crowded.
In this journey to recovery, I feel desolation.

My prayers seemed to go unanswered. My parents believed that suffering is an inevitable part of life and hidden in the pain are seeds for renewal. Richard Rohr, a Franciscan priest, offers words of wisdom, *"All great spirituality is about what we do with our pain. If we do not transform our pain, we will transmit it to those around us"* (Spirituality and Practice, n.d.). Sadly, at this early stage of my recovery, I projected my suffering onto those around me. My family was living in another period of crisis, but my mother held firm: *"Our faith kept our hope alive making us stronger to deal with Kathy's resistance to recognize the far-reaching consequences of brain injury."*

Medical research has recently acknowledged that spirituality or faith in a Divine presence can reduce fear by providing hope, which is considered an inherent part of being a conscious human being. Hope is also known to be a protective and strengthening factor in healing. However, for the first time in my life, I doubted my relationship with God and could not understand why this chain of events had happened to me. The depth of my doubt was evident in my resistance to accept what could not be changed. Dealing with future uncertainty caused indescribable feelings of agitation.

When I believed I had nothing to offer others, I sank deeper into depression. My self-esteem and confidence disappeared. It seemed like everything was distorted including a positive sense of myself in relationship with others. I was still being prescribed non-habit-forming antidepressants to help improve my mood. When the end of year two arrived, Dr. Franklyn noted *"Kathy experiences typical mood changes associated with grief, loss, and emotional adjustment. Her New Year's Eve was uneventful, and she felt alone – depressed – angry...I reminded her of her faith/belief system, and she was uplifted (January 4, 1995).* As a medical professional she recognized my deep spiritual beliefs could ease the suffering from extreme loss. When asked if I wanted to hold on to my 'religious philosophies', I said yes, but since the crash I did not know how: *"Kathy is finding it difficult to reconcile her new (less inhibited) thoughts and behaviours with her previous life as a nun."*

Being at home I really missed the joy I received from the social life of my St. Anne community as my days revolved around appointments and caregivers. I felt disconnected without my teaching community. I could not envision a meaningful purpose in my new circumstances. My self-confidence disappeared and I had doubts of being lovable. My life was on a roller-coaster as the feelings of powerlessness dragged on.

Hope and Wisdom

Thankfully, my parents continually tried to remind me that things would get better in God's time, giving me fleeting moments of hope. They believed something positive would eventually come out of the crisis we were living. The many wisdom stories presented in the Bible about healing the 'broken hearted' and the 'binding of wounds' (Psalm 147:3) were inspiring to me before the crash. Now it was personal, and I had to be reminded how far I had come from death's door. On a very deep level I wanted to rediscover my inner pathway to the source of peace and happiness. As Dr. Franklyn predicted in several of our sessions, *"This will be more difficult than she anticipates."* (November 24, 1993), (September 28, 1994). My mind was blocked, and I was unable to comprehend the emotional, physical, mental, and spiritual damage being caused by holding onto resentment, anger, and hate. It took years for me to recognize the effects of my distorted, negative thinking.

My psychologist was a godsend to my recovery. Her patient efforts and challenging questions influenced my thinking so I could respond to life's challenges in a much more positive manner. I needed to take responsibility and consider the impact of my behaviour on others who might need inspiration instead of disparagement. One day she asked me to make a list of blessings, redirecting my woeful thoughts onto the pathway of loving compassion. I needed to be reminded that the source of healing was resting within me. But opening my heart so I could once again be in touch with my inner spiritual self would take a renewed faith in possibilities.

Dr. Franklyn's compassionate understanding to gently confront misconceptions helped me survive the depths of depression. Each week her holistic approach was lifesaving as she helped me re-learn how to problem-solve and move through the huge mountain of obstacles. Relentlessly she reinforced a realistic and optimistic perspective to ease the intense anxiety I was facing so I could reconnect to the resilient qualities that characterized the old Kathy. When I was stuck on hopelessness, she often reminded me that I had been an accomplished educator who deeply cared for people. After two years in recovery, my brain was beginning to forge new pathways so the interpersonal skills I mastered long ago became accessible. I did not realize it at the time but the ability to truly understand deep pain would eventually be a blessing to comfort others in despair. Years later in an art class I painted a picture of an imagined 'Tree of Hope'. I used various colours on each branch to illustrate the many problem-solving opportunities that can help the brain heal from TBI.

Painting of my 'Tree of Hope'

Part IV

Transition

"Holding on is believing that there's only a past; letting go is knowing there's a future." Daphne Rose Kingma

A period of transition is a passageway filled with opportunities for growth and healing in a time of major upheaval. As year 3 was approaching the fog of confusion was dissipating and I was moving along the road of recovery toward a deeper level of consciousness. Milestones were in reach to recognize the extent of loss so I could give myself permission to grieve. Trying to understand the entangled legalities I was in became a major hurdle to move forward.

I was interested in reading expert opinions used by insurance companies and felt threatened because I was convinced the cards to provide future financial security were stacked against me. Thankfully my father requested documentation at every step and kept meticulous records. He had a routine to submit claims in a timely manner, however the car insurance company was habitually tardy. My savings and teachers' disability benefit helped keep me afloat. I had mortgage payments and the usual bills, so I became easily panicked when I thought about not being able to cover future day-to-day living expenses. This was something I never had to deal with before the crash.

As my parents dealt with lawyers, insurance companies and my union representative, the ongoing uncertainty of my financial future created unmanageable stress, worry and anxiety. It started nine months after the crash when Dr. Franklyn recognized that I was emotionally and physically unfit to attend court for discovery proceedings. Her letter stating disapproval was supported by the Director of the Regional Rehabilitation Centre and preliminaries went ahead without my attendance. When arguments about the cause of events were presented, my Dad heard the police report that a young man driving a Blazer was late for a mid-term exam at the University of Windsor and ran through a red light. An accident reconstruction company presented their findings in 1995 describing the crash as an 'accident':

> *We understand that this accident occurred at approximately 8:05 a.m. on 24 February 1993. A 1991 Ford Escort driven by Ms. Labbe (my maiden name) was eastbound on Highway 2 at Lesperance Road in Sandwich South Township, Essex County, Ontario. Ms. Labbe intended to turn left to travel northbound on Lesperance Road. However, partway through the turn, her vehicle became involved in a collision with a westbound 1986 S10 Blazer driven by (a young man, name withheld).*
>
> *The Escort sustained collision damage concentrated to its right front corner, substantial crushing of the fender, bumper, rad support, and hood. The top of the right front wheel had been pushed towards the car. Ms. Labbe suffered injuries as a result of this accident.*
>
> *The Blazer sustained collision damage concentrated to the front end. The left half of the bumper had crushed rearwards into the left fender crumpled in an accordion fashion. The left side of the hood was displaced rearwards to left rear quarter panel immediately rearward of the driver's door...The environmental conditions are documented as being clear daylight, and the pavement is characterized as having been dry asphalt in good condition.*

There was no mention of injuries to the other driver in the report. Our local newspaper reported the crash and requested eyewitnesses to come forward and that the young man driving the Blazer was *"treated and released for a minor knee injury."*

It is common for people to refer to what happened on that day as an accident. The word 'accident' is defined as an unexpected event typically sudden in nature associated with injury, loss, or harm. In other words, events that happen *could not* be prevented. On the other hand, a 'motor vehicle collision', commonly called a 'crash', is a destructive event that *could have been* prevented. Policy writers and experts in law enforcement, medicine, and injury prevention have acknowledged the necessity to make this important distinction to improve safety and accurately reflect the reality of what happens. Prevention means taking appropriate precautions and by being aware of one's actions and surrounding environment. Protective safety measures such as wearing a seat belt, proper vehicle maintenance etc. may improve outcomes of unfortunate preventable events. Risks taken because of a few seconds of impatience, among other factors, can result in untold devastation that will change lives forever. The truth is, I was in a preventable 'motor vehicle collision' that caused multiple life-changing wounds. It was not an accident. My body, mind and spirit would never be completely restored to the healthy condition it was moments before.

Assigning blame was being argued as partly my fault because forensic evidence suggested I did not have my seat belt on. A bank receipt confirmed I made a stop that was only a few miles away. Additional questions surfaced that perhaps in my haste to get to school I might not have put my seat belt back on. When this possibility was initially raised, I was outraged at this accusation because it was never my habit. Dr. Franklyn noted that hostile impulses became more erratic and needed to be addressed immediately.

Each step of the legal process contributed to anticipatory anxiety causing a range of irrational behaviours. At one point I picked up a treasured two-inch oak wooden stool made by my Dad and in rage slammed it down breaking it in half. When I realized what I had done I broke down and cried thinking if someone had been in my path, I would have killed them. I did not know how to get rid of the deep hate that lived inside of me. Talk therapy with Dr. Franklyn and externalizing blame to whomever would listen, helped to release internal tension but it became an unhealthy vicious cycle that took years to let go.

Career or Vocation

There was also the question of future 'career' possibilities, which is a common expectation. I was obsessed with returning to my school community and the vocation I loved. When exploring different roles within education, my principal told me that in time, it may be possible to return as a teacher's assistant. Then I was advised by the union representative that I would have to remain in the teachers' union or lose health and pension benefits. Going back to St. Anne's as a tutor, campus minister or even a teacher's assistant did not appear sensible options. I became extremely frustrated with the lack of teaching options available and became discouraged that I was in this situation.

As ongoing discussions about a career change were taking place with the insurance company, pressure was being increased to be retrained and I had to go through six hours of 'vocational testing'. The results revealed sustained problems in organization and memory that would be problematic in a work setting. This only led to intense fear that I would end up working in a fast-food restaurant becoming an ongoing issue discussed with Dr. Franklyn. There was no reasoning with me and the source of all my problems went right back to blaming the guy who caused my accident. I felt that my circumstances would not bother me so much if I could figure out ways to have him killed. Then I would argue with myself, writing, *"Okay, maybe not kill him but harm him so he would feel the same emotional and physical pain as I am."*

The hate I had for that driver ran deep for many years. I was wrestling with the conflict inside myself because I was reconciling my new less inhibited thoughts and behaviours with my spiritual beliefs. Despite wanting to resist the thoughts that came into my head, I couldn't let the negativity go. The rumination felt so real and was devastating to my mental health and I brought my concerns to Dr. Franklyn: *"Very upset today about the past week's occurrences. Kathy tends to ruminate about things and relates everything to her injury. Feeling helpless and worried ...very upset about forms to be completed etc. She needs to practice her strategies more consistently, e.g. Who can solve this or assist me here?"*

When the insurance company began discussions to terminate funding the expense for my psychologist, she successfully argued for continued counselling: *"Kathy is not at all ready to consider this. She considers our sessions her opportunity to 'regroup', organize her thoughts, emotions, etc. and plan for her future. She needs to make sense of what is happening to her weekly as well as to ensure that she moves along the continuum to independence."* As I lingered in a vicious cycle of anger and resentment, I knew that I desperately needed her help. There were many obstacles that were still unidentified blocking my quest for independence, peace, and happiness. It was a complicated and confusing period of not being able to understand my changed circumstances or the impact on my entire being.

Grief and Loss

It was time to give myself permission to grieve, not only because of my debilitating situation but the cumulative loss being endured by my entire family. Grief was complicated as we were each harbouring deep sorrow from the premature death of my younger sister Myra. She was a very kind and considerate person who always took care of everyone instead of taking time out from her busy schedule to care for her own health. Myra was my sister and friend. Her compassionate spirit has never left me, and I knew she would understand the depth of my grief. I lost so much of myself and desperately wanted to reclaim my former life. The challenges before me were overwhelming and I did not trust God to help me move out of the misery I was living. So, I often turned to Myra's spirit, silently sharing my feelings of uncertainty, and sorrow. I asked her to watch over our entire family and give me the strength that I needed to move on.

Grief also affected dear friends who were heart broken when they heard that I had a slim chance to survive or return to my former self. My dear friend Jeannie traveled from Montreal to visit me and wrote about her own grief:

> *From a personal standpoint I had to grieve the loss of my friend. She didn't die, but the Kathy I knew, was gone. The relationship we once had before the crash had changed. For many years, her focus was solely on her health and the trauma from the subsequent on-going court case. This meant that for a long time she couldn't engage with any depth in reciprocal relationship building...Healthy relationships evolve and grow. We have had to learn that there is give and take around expectations when brain injury is the culprit.*

I now understand that I was unable to be present. The 'old Kathy' was gone, and the 'new Kathy' was consumed in simply trying to survive. I was unable to fully comprehend the extent of loss and my limitations so I could move forward. My grief was like being in a chaotic twirling cone moving up and down between rational thought, socially acceptable behaviour and angry outbursts fueled by mounting emotions of frustration. Everything appeared complicated and when I needed the comfort of my faith to pull me through, I lacked belief. Gradually, a spark of recognition was ignited that real change must come from the inside of me. I do not remember the exact moment when I slipped beyond the veil of despair, but I do remember that a major shift was occurring when I became filled with a renewed spirit, one of hope.

Transitioning into Acceptance

A third neuro-psychological report was prepared for the insurance company on May 12th, 1995, building on prior reports and new information. Progress was made in certain areas, but I was still a long way from being functionally independent. Obstacles stemming from my brain injury and physical pain were identified and I struggled with making sense of my new reality: *"Kathy does not understand why she cannot drive and that parents need to hold onto her driver's license for now."* Dr. Franklyn was helping me process what the words "for now" meant. I entered a period of transition when I was able to put professional opinions about my strengths and weaknesses into the light of logic. This change in thinking was vital to moving forward in my healing.

Perhaps my natural stubborn streak or my internal wisdom helped me recognize that I had to dedicate myself to the work ahead so I could rewire my brain and push beyond my limitations, what the medical world called 'deficits'. In the hospital I was repeatedly told in many different words, that I had to accept my circumstances. Was that the truth? I believed in the wise Chinese proverb, *"That a journey of a thousand miles begins with a single step."* I could either dwell on suffering with a negative attitude and languish in a world of my own illusions or face the hard work of developing a positive attitude and perspective. The fog that was clouding full consciousness was lifting. Slowly, I began to realize certain impairments could be altered if I worked on my weak cognitive areas. I was being encouraged to do something about changing my situation in the belief that surprising opportunities would surface. However not everyone had the same opinion. With every defeating statement I quietly replied, *"Just watch me!"*

Survive or Thrive

Becoming a survivor was the primary goal for the medical team tending to my care and I am forever grateful. I was very fortunate to have six years of weekly sessions with my psychologist paid for, which was a critical factor in my recovery. She helped me recognize my role in the healing process. I not only wanted to survive I wanted to thrive as a fully self-reliant and independent functioning adult. As elusive as it seemed at the time, I needed to tackle some of the obstacles that were staring at me in the doctor's report.

Reading between the lines I began to realize that I had to deal with victimhood fueling my anger. This is a major hurdle in recovery (Kaufman, 2020). This meant I would have to be lovingly but firmly confronted. Because I trusted Dr. Franklyn, I gave her permission to challenge me. It was not easy being told that there was another way to look at things and it was my perception of reality that was dragging me down. Accepting her suggestions was often a struggle, but I always left her office thinking about what she said. When I ruminated about something I did not agree with, my negative opinion would weave itself into conversations that followed until I had an uh-huh moment and recognized the wisdom in her advice.

The trait of being stubborn was a gift when I was able to maintain a calm and kind presence. It is a strength that serves me to create positive change; but there is a flip side. Being close-minded, rejecting others' ideas and becoming angry when things do not go my way not only harmed myself but also impacted important relationships in my life. When contentious situations surfaced, my overblown reactions were labelled as part of the impaired 'personality functioning' that I needed to come to terms with. F*** O** was always on the tip of my tongue. I had to learn how to control my words and the anger that could be triggered from a simple misunderstanding.

I knew that my brain injury caused short-term memory problems, a casualty from the damage to the pre-frontal cortex of my brain. I had extreme difficulty following instructions or staying focused to finish what I started. Distractions had me retracing my steps time and time again as I muttered, *"What was I just doing?"* I also tended to repeat myself, forgetting what I already said or asking for something to be repeated causing some people to become annoyed. It bothered me so much that I regularly spoke to Dr. Franklyn about this concern. She suggested that instead of going on the defensive when someone had a perplexed look on their face, simply ask, "Did you hear me say this before?" Learning how to read body language and not taking things personally are other issues I still try to overcome.

Physical limitations added to my frustration. The surgery on my knee, right tibia and fused right toe continue to give me problems and pain especially when rain is in the air. The coupe-contrecoup blow to my head caused complicated auditory problems resulting in numerous misunderstandings that are also common to TBI. When I couldn't hear properly, I would simply tune out and stop following the conversation. Today I am now wearing hearing aids for high pitch frequency loss which helps. Depth perception is still distorted when I get into a bathtub or use stairs, so I rely on sturdy bars and railings. Going down steps is even worse because looking at something that is descending appears distorted. As the steps seem to blend, it is difficult to differentiate where one step ends and another begins. At times, the uncertainty causes overwhelming fear where my knees begin to tremble, and my vision loses focus. The last thing I want to do is fall or further injure my leg.

When I was visiting relatives in Peggy's Cove, my cousin wanted to walk on the rocks to get a better view. With reassurance that she would hold onto me I held her hand like a vice grip. It was not fun at all. On another occasion I was seated in a balcony at a concert and when I had to get up, I was terrorized. I could not move my legs. I was overwhelmed by feelings that I was going to fall. With my cousin on one side and an usher on the other I managed to get down the steps. When that episode was over, the fear settled into deep resentment that something so simple was taken away from me.

Subtle Spiritual Connections

I now realize that influence to change course can be subtle. My circle of care expanded beyond medical professionals and my family. Social support played a critical role as I began to adjust to the new reality of the adversity I was facing. I started to realize that I was surrounded by people who had faith, believing that healing and the unfolding of my life will come through a spiritual connection. My parents prayed every day that I would get better. My dear SNJM community believed that things would eventually get better even though my mind was filled with discouragement. They sent faith filled prayers and reflections by email that spoke to me, uplifting my spirits. I was being reminded over and over that the Divine Spirit is there in the shadows of the chaotic storm I was in. Restoring my own belief and faith in the certainty that there is a loving God would take time. I was in shifting sands, and little by little I was beginning to recover my spiritual self, able to trust in a world of possibilities once again.

Encouraged to take responsibility for making my relationships work, I was being reminded time and time again that I had to be compassionate to myself and quiet the obsessive thoughts of blame toward the other driver. I spent years ruminating by imagining terrible punishments as he continued along with his life, basically unchanged and unharmed. Even the thought that I would have to take partial responsibility for not wearing a seat belt caused intense anger. I carried the burden of resentment for the eleven years that it took before his insurance company awarded a settlement for pain and suffering. Worrying about things that were not in my control drained my energy and made me weaker.

Dr. Franklyn challenged my tendencies when I wandered down the road of negative defeating thoughts. She helped me recognize that I had to be the guardian of my own thinking and not be deceived in dwelling on discouraging events by blowing things out of proportion. At the centre of all my frustration was blaming the other driver. I was often reminded to refocus my negativity by repeating the affirmation, *"Do not give away my power to him."* I was being asked to work on stopping the negative chattering of my incessant mind. I needed to 'change the channel' back to the spiritual teachings I grew up with. This strategy would help my injured brain begin healing itself back into the positive person I once was.

Letting go of the vicious cycle of hate, resentment, and anger was the most difficult step in my recovery. Aware of my Roman Catholic upbringing, Dr. Franklyn tried many times to reinforce a core spiritual belief to unconditionally 'love one's enemies as oneself'. She offered suggestions on how to change my heart and thinking but I was unable and perhaps not ready to hear her wisdom: *"Forgiveness of the other person is needed if she is to move on"* (July 6-20, 1995). Forgiving the other driver who ran a red light causing my crash did not require a face-to-face intervention. There would be no apology or punishment and the monetary restitution would never be enough. Little did I know that the healing power of forgiveness was going to take a very long time to surface.

Conflicts and transgressions in life are unavoidable. I was unable to grasp the meaning of forgiveness even though it is a fundamental belief in my Christian tradition as with many other religions. I would never meet the other driver as warnings were issued not to have face-to-face contact. I wondered if quietly forgiving him would eliminate the deep resentment and dark thoughts for revenge. Ruminating was stressful making me feel angry, sad, anxious, and less in control. These are all negative, unhealthy, emotional states. The longer I didn't change my thinking, the larger the toll on my physical, mental, social, and spiritual health. Alternatively, forgiveness offers a port in the storm I was living. Peace was possible if I was able to make a conscious decision not to "give away my power to him." I was trying to understand that freedom from the anguish could be found in the willingness to 'let go'. I was listening to my wise psychologist when I wrote this poem but this step in my recovery would take a very long time.

Alone in my Search for Freedom

I have choices as I search for a lamp
to light the way
not here nor there but within.
Discovering the still quiet place
to rest in the light and listen:
"Kathy! You hold the key to willingness
that will get you out
of that prison of darkness.
Then and only then will you be free."

The Power of Positive Thinking

Inspirational sayings uplifted my darkened spirits and reminded me to see adversity through a positive lens. Addiction is common to TBI and mine was food. I also knew how important a good diet was if I wanted to get better. Each week I attended a Weight Watchers' group that had positive messaging themes. Meetings began with a gentle challenge intended to build up self-confidence so members can live a happy and fulfilling life. One simple saying became my morning prayer:

Face it 'till you make it!

Get up. Work hard. Fail. Stand back up.

Face it again!

The fluctuation in my weight was a crazy-making roller coaster ride over the years, negatively impacting my self-esteem. In my mind I continued to see myself as the 'fat kid' who was made fun of, part of a pre-existing condition that my sub-conscious held onto to. It took me a very long time to realize that programs, such as Weight Watchers, are not just about counting calories but changing your perspective. As I continued to open myself to share my insecurities and fear, Dr. Franklyn helped me to see how I was changing. At a deep level I needed to learn how to have self-compassion and love myself before I could love others: *"Good things happened this week. Kathy had experiences that made her feel loved. She is now realizing that she is capable of being loved. She is becoming more consistent in dealing with moods/anger adaptively. She uses the techniques taught ...they are working."*

Collage of affirmations in my weight journey

Discovering Motivation

Boredom was still a problem and very difficult to deal with when I had a lot of time on my hands. My thoughts were on a roller coaster and when I wasn't doing something worthwhile, I started thinking that I might have been better off dead raising alarm bells for Dr. Franklyn. She encouraged me to start volunteering at Windsor Western Hospital's rehabilitation floor and sit with patients at lunchtime. I was still connected to my school community and was invited to return and talk with students. I was starting to think more about possibilities on how to access my work-related experience to help myself and others.

Despite others thinking I was a dreamer, my daily thoughts were filled with possibilities of teaching and driving again. I became realistic about my limitations and turned my resentment into a plan of action. The affirmation "Success is the best revenge" was sinking in. I was motivated to work on my short-term memory and regain the knowledge lost to me. I recognized that I needed to go back to school, which was a humbling experience. After being a high school teacher for eight years I returned to the Adult Learning Centre from 1994-1996 and enrolled as an adult student to study grade 9 English and Math. When I walked into my first English class, two former students who had dropped out of high school were also there wondering what I was doing sitting in a seat rather than at the front of the room. I held it together, explaining I was learning just like them because I had a brain injury from a car crash. That moment was so unsettling that I cried when I went home. Tears did not come easy to me.

My first math test was also very emotional. My eyes would not focus on the paper and the room started spinning. My compassionate teacher recognized my agitation and gave me time to settle myself down, letting me write the test after everyone left. She arranged a university student to tutor me who happened to be a former peer helper in my life skills class. I too was a tutor in statistics when I went to university. I was grateful for her assistance, but terrible feelings of inadequacy washed over me drawing me further into deep depression. The never-ending question of "Why me?" went unanswered. Again, I felt abandoned by God, stuck in my own miserable thoughts without answers.

After this particularly depressive episode, I remember waking up from my dreams determined to get involved in the life of the school as I had done when I was a teacher at St. Anne's. Socializing helped me feel accepted despite my limitations. I joined the 'student council' during a letter writing campaign against the pending closing of the Adult Learning Centre. I had gratitude for the many opportunities that became available. I helped type the letters that went to the school board and local MPPs. I also volunteered to follow up with telephone calls. With encouragement I spoke at a school board meeting representing the students. Our efforts did not prevent the school from closing shortly after I left. It took many years for this decision to be reversed, so I like to believe that we eventually influenced the outcome.

My self-esteem was improving because I was contributing to an important cause. I felt empowered by getting back into my old routine as an advocate for the underdog. I was developing 'cognitive flexibility' by identifying small attainable goals and using my stubborn tendencies as an advantage. When the graduation ceremony was held at the Adult Learning Centre, I proudly joined my former St. Anne's students. I was successful in all my classes, and I received a pin in recognition of my perseverance and leadership. I was making progress and I felt gratitude for being honoured for my contributions to the life of the school.

Navigating Toward Independence

Driving has always represented freedom to me. While still in a fog, I often talked about being able to drive again so I could regain control over my life. I also wanted to follow my passion of helping others, so getting around to volunteer on my own time was essential to me. The desire to get behind the wheel of an automobile seemed very strange to most people. Dr. Franklyn tried to keep things in perspective with reassurance that I was making progress whenever my obsession to drive came up:

> *Driving is seen as a major barrier to independence and improved self-esteem. She is sick and tired of depending on others to provide transportation...Right now, I am trying to assist Kathy in reflecting on events of the past two years and in particular her progress so she consistently sees herself as moving onward (May 10th and 19th, 1995).*

I tended to forget the small steps I was making in recovery. My best friend from Grade 9, Jean Tousignant came to visit me often and witnessed the progressive changes over two years:

> *Once she was able to have visitors, my husband and I drove to Windsor to visit Kathy in the hospital. I certainly wasn't prepared*

for our visit. There she was lying in a hospital bed looking so disorientated and helpless. She also kept saying that the nurses were mean to her and not taking care of her and she wanted to go home. I felt my heart was breaking into a million pieces. All I wanted to do was give her a big hug and tell her that everything was going to be okay. As soon as we got back into the car, I couldn't stop crying. All I could think is that Kathy would never be the same again and that she would need someone to take care of her for the rest of her life. In a split second, her life changed forever.

She showed everyone, the doctors, the nurses, family, and friends, that this would not keep her down. She had to relearn how to walk, talk, feed herself, but gradually with everything she had within herself and with the grace of God, she was able to go home. I remember the first time I went to visit her at her house, there were yellow post-it notes all over to help with her memory. At first, she had to have health care workers and after some time passed, she became more independent.

More time passed and she told me that she wanted her licence back. I couldn't believe what I was hearing. After the total nightmare that she went through, she wanted to drive again! Even though I was shocked and couldn't even imagine her wanting to get behind the wheel of a car again, I understood that Kathy was tired of depending on taxis to take her places and she wanted her independence back. Shame on me for not having more faith in my friend.

My stubborn mind was made up and I was going to be proactive to move toward this goal. After the third neuropsychological testing, I had the nerve to question the doctor's opinion that prohibited me from being reinstated as an independent driver. When I asked if I could drive, he said *"No, you are not ready."* I was very upset and built up the nerve to ask him if he worked for the Ministry of Transportation. I argued, *"Why don't you send me to the Ministry of Transportation and let them make the decision."* Surprisingly the doctor turned to my case coordinator, Sue Rendall Hannon, requesting that she investigate the availability to be assessed at the Hugh McMillan Rehabilitation Centre in Toronto. Procedural steps had to be followed based on individual needs and abilities before recommending adaptive equipment, special instruction, extended waiting period for more recovery time or a restoration of driving privileges with conditions.

Hoops to Drive Through

With the doctor's recommendation to 'attempt' the program, I was accepted as a candidate so travelled by train to Toronto with my mother on June 26, 1995. We took a cab to the Rehabilitation Driving Assessment Centre where I attended an in-class session to determine my physical ability and visual skills in areas such as depth perception, field of awareness, colour, glare recovery, and night vision. I also had a peripheral vision test done by keeping my head stationary with a wooden disc under my nose. When a round orange circle appeared in my line of vision, I had to acknowledge that I could see it. Cognitive skills were measured to determine my ability to manage the rules of the road.

The Brake and Steering Reaction Test was done in a simulator car with brake pedals. I had to pretend I was driving using the pedals to respond correctly to the green, orange, and red traffic lights. The trained instructor kept track of my distance judgement and reaction time giving special attention to my injured right leg. In the afternoon, I had an hour-long assessment with an instructor who was trained to test people with TBI in a car customized with vehicle modifications. First, I adjusted the seat and mirrors appropriately. I was unfamiliar with the gas and brake pedals so I tended to speed by putting too much pressure on the gas but that improved before the end of the session. I was a little nervous, but I knew I could drive despite not being behind the wheel for more than two years.

I gained confidence after I finally realized the car crash was not my fault although I may have contributed to my injury by not having a seat belt on. I was determined to show the evaluator that I was a good candidate to return to driving. The initial report from Hugh McMillan Rehabilitation Centre stated I had the potential to return to driving and identified areas I needed to work on before coming back for a second assessment:

> *When coached regarding the proper use of her eyes, Kathy's steering and right and left-hand turns improved a great deal. She consistently made good decisions and positioned herself well for turns. Kathy tended to exceed the speed limit and will need to work on this area. At intersections, she needs to increase the amount of scanning the environment and requires some practice when following and meeting traffic. Her tracking while driving was somewhat "off", however, it seems workable and did improve*

with coaching. Throughout the session Kathy was receptive to coaching and instructions and seems eager to return to driving.

(June 26,1995; Jennifer Wigle BSc (O.T.) Drivers Rehabilitation Services, The Hugh McMillan Rehabilitation Centre)

The next day I talked to Dr. Franklyn: "*Kathy received good news! She was told that some spatial and vision problems persist, but she should be able to improve her skills in ten lessons. She will arrange this in a few months.*" The drawback to get my license reinstated was a mandatory time limit of three months set by the Ministry of Transportation for the lessons and final assessment to be successfully completed. Otherwise, my license would be suspended permanently.

Over the next three months I was stressed waiting for the ministry to get back to me. During my sessions with Dr. Franklyn, I was irritated and started venting over things I could not do myself around the house. I was frustrated over little things such my Dad cutting my grass on his time. It sounds ridiculous now, but I was focused on things being done so I didn't have to think about it anymore. I also tended to raise my voice, arguing with my sister when she came over to clean. I could not understand why she found my reactions offensive, and I felt she should understand my TBI condition better. I had a bag of mixed feelings and often had regret over my inability to cooperate. Targeting my family was a still a major problem I needed to overcome. Dr. Franklyn noted that I was unwilling to consider alternatives after she offered the suggestion to hire someone other than family to do household chores that were physically difficult for me:

Kathy has not regained all her problem-solving abilities... Discussed preoccupation with self and how this tendency affects a person's emotional state, interpersonal and vocational relationships as well as perceptions of reality. (July 6-20, 1995)

It was evident that I continued to have a very difficult time with TBI symptoms. Whenever I tried to argue about perceived injustice, my psychologist consistently tried to re-frame my negative thinking into a positive way of looking at things:

Asked Kathy to list positive changes since initial accident. Suggested she write down some of these things to reflect upon when she is down. When things go wrong, Kathy tends to resort to seeing herself as a burden and forgets her progress...needs to have this repeated several times. She interprets everything negatively until alternatives are pointed out. (July & August 1995)

To combat the entrenchment of negative pathways she reminded me that in the past I had the strength to deal with difficult situations. Getting my license reinstated was one of those times. The affirmation she so often repeated, "Do what you have to do" echoed in my mind and helped to further my determination. There was evidence of progress when she helped me to return to the deep well of optimistic resilience that seemed to be quietly resting deep in my long-term memory. I would often imagine myself driving again and recalled feelings of freedom to have control over the activities of my day.

I returned to Toronto in August 1995 for three days of training and final testing. This was an expensive venture that included transportation, accommodation, and the cost of the program. Thankfully expenses were approved by the insurance company with the support of my case coordinator. Training included planning a route and driving independently using proper signalling and stopping techniques without coaching. I drove in residential areas for two days then progressed to busier roads including the Gardiner Expressway. Wow was I ever nervous, but I was excited to be driving and I wanted to show the instructor that I had the ability and confidence to drive safely on the road again.

The final step was passing a three-part evaluation with a written portion, a vision test, and a driving component. A test track was set up with several streets for special testing behind the Brampton Ministry of Transportation office. The assessment officer had a remote control that activated various scenarios to test my response. There was a railroad crossing where she could activate signals and a one-way street. When the tester asked me to reverse directions by doing a three-point turn, I told her I couldn't because I would end up going in the wrong direction, which was the right answer! When she had me go back to the building and park the car, she told me to go in and get my license stamped. I passed all three tests and had my license reinstated!!

I was so excited! Two and a half years after the crash results were sent to the Ministry of Transportation, my insurance company, lawyer, case coordinator and three of my doctors who had the last say on medical fitness. I was qualified to drive but I did not have enough money to buy a car until a year later, so I still had to rely on taxis, buses, and others to get me where I wanted to go. But I felt I had passed over a threshold and could start making my own decisions. Sister Helen Petrimoulx provided a reflection on this stage of my healing journey:

> *Kathy at this point in her journey, defines for me, what real 'determination' looks like. With gritty resolve and will power she*

fought through each day, and this brought back the Kathy I knew and love. I witnessed her move through the many struggles and obstacles to achieve victory over such a serious brain injury. She was pure inspiration teaching me to never give up. She shared her dreams with me that one day, she would be able to drive a car again and I saw her joy as this happened. I just shook my head in awe and watched in wonder, 'What's the next goal I will surely witness?'

Return to Post-Secondary Education

When my focus returned to teaching, I would start off each day thinking, *"Do what I need to do."* The next best route to further upgrade the skills and knowledge I acquired long ago was a return to college. Before becoming a teacher, I earned a diploma in Business Administration with a focus on accounting and a certificate in Ontario Management. I worked at three different business jobs that were not fulfilling. The insurance companies' expectations to return to work was always on my mind. There was hope that my long-term memory would be triggered for success, lining up with the retraining agenda so I would be an employable candidate in an alternative career, which was not my plan. The insurance company paid for me to be enrolled in the Office Administration General and Executive programs between 1996 and 2000. I worked hard at overcoming cognitive problems, but frustration often bubbled over.

Things were going well but holding onto resentment lingered and demonstrating socially acceptable behaviour continued to be a challenge. When I felt overwhelmed with the way the lessons were being taught, I often lashed out with criticism making my brain injury issues the teacher's problem. When I simply did not understand what I was being asked to do the teacher would send me to the Learning Disability Office. In hindsight the teacher was simply trying to do her best managing the classroom and pace of the lesson. Every week I shared my school experience with Dr. Franklyn who helped me develop strategies so I could handle the emotions generated from interpersonal conflict and not explode. But recalling the strategies in the moment was a different story. Exams and fear of not passing were triggers difficult to control the entire time I was in college: *"Kathy was upset because she spoke inappropriately to a teacher. The inhibition problem persists!"* (November 24, 1995, October 22, 1997).

Anxiety obscured my self-defeating perception. I needed to increase my awareness of potential triggers so I could choose alternative 'kinder' ways of thinking. It was not easy to accept my psychologist's suggestions and it took significant effort to reconsider that she was offering sound professional advice and not hear her words as criticism. I trusted Dr. Franklyn with my vulnerabilities by discussing ongoing interpersonal issues that caused anger problems. With considerable patience she helped me learn how to bring situations under control: *"Breathe and reconsider."* To calm down I also tried to change the 'channels in my mind' so I could I remember that there are so many blessings to be thankful for.

A frustrating learning curve occurred using adaptive technology for note taking. Organizing myself also remained problematic. Dr. Franklyn worked as a go-between with the claims representative so I could get a day-timer intended to be user-friendly for brain injury victims. It had a place for inserts and ribbons to divide various sections for telephone numbers and appointments. Bulky with a cumbersome zipper it just increased my frustration.

Routine memory enhancement strategies were continually reinforced by Dr. Franklyn. We found the humour in some incidents because there were times after searching for something, I would find the item right in front of me. After one frustrating episode of finding my keys right next to the milk in the fridge, I became focused on 'everything has a place' and developed better habits of putting things away in my house. Post-it notes were everywhere. But other times such as losing an $85.00 textbook, I slid back into a vicious despondent cycle repeatedly saying the dreaded words, "I am so stupid." By putting things in perspective, she helped me realize that even if something is lost, things can be replaced.

When TBI issues surfaced, or I had setbacks thinking that teaching would never again be possible, I often became very emotional and irrational:

> *Kathy tends to ruminate about things and relates everything to her injury ...gets upset about forms to be completed etc., easily overwhelmed. I stressed that she needs to practice her problem-solving strategies more consistently, e.g. 'Who can solve or assist me here' ...Anger is more subtle but presents as sarcasm. Social interaction difficulties continue to surface. Reminded her that she needs to stop using 'all or none' statements. (January-May 1996)*

I was continuing to express egocentricity, a self-centred tendency that is typical in some cases of TBI. I was adamant at times that everyone else needed to change to my way of thinking instead of realizing it was I who needed to adapt. It was a struggle to realize that I could not have my own way all the time, which meant I still needed to continue working on cognitive flexibility to better control my inappropriate responses. I was doing well in all my courses with assistance, so I held onto the feasibility of returning to work as a teacher. However, Dr. Franklyn could see the reality of my situation noting: *"Kathy and I spoke again about the feasibility of returning to work as a teacher/educator. She still slips back and forth into 'fantasy' regarding this idea" (January 1996).*

Another Compassionate Advocate

Behind the scenes Dr. Franklyn was working with June Egan, a compassionate staff member in the Learning Disability Office so I could receive support in my course work and assessments such as tests and exams. June Egan never gave up on me and knew how to calm me down. She recognized that under my aggressive behaviour was potential and she continually advocated on my behalf. She also recommended that I join the Disability Committee, and other opportunities came my way. I was recovering my thoughtful calm voice when I was able to speak for the disadvantaged. As a 'student representative' I attended different forums and conferences that examined programming from a disabled person's point of view. I was often asked to debrief with college decision-makers, sharing my impressions and what I learned at the numerous functions I attended. I felt that my input was valued helping to improve my low self-esteem.

A very powerful experience was my role of companion to a student in a wheelchair. We were going to Ottawa by train, and I was entrusted to remind the conductors that he required special accommodations to ensure safety and assistance to move between the transfer points along the route. I was making new friends and I was reaching out to help others. Giving freely from the heart helped me to experience the joy of committing random acts of kindness. I was experiencing the wisdom of Chinese and Biblical proverbs, that the more one gives, the more one has. Once again, I was validated by my psychologist.

Days of Celebration

On May 28th, 1996, I bought a new purple Ford Focus and shared my joy with everyone. I saw it as my ticket to get more involved in volunteering and participate as a functional adult in the outside world. The car insurance company required that I take two additional lessons with Young Canada Driving School because I had not driven my own automobile since 1993. I felt a little embarrassed taking lessons, but I did it. When my two lessons were done, my first trip by myself was to Devonshire Mall. The freedom of being a window shopper by simply walking with my cane was thrilling. I became more mobile and independent relieving the feelings of being frustrated and a burden to others.

I could feel Spirit's light beginning to shine in the darkness when I made a conscious decision to work on changing my negative outlook. When I was successful at St. Clair College, I felt deep gratitude for all the people who reached out and saw beyond my physical, mental, and emotional disabilities. The day finally came for my college graduation ceremony on June 19th, 1998. I felt so proud of 'our' accomplishments when Dr. Franklyn accepted my invitation to walk with me up the steps and across the stage to receive my Office Administration General diploma. My entire family attended the celebration along with my staunch supporter and dear friend Sister Emma. I continued my college education until June 2000 and earned a specialist in Executive Administration. My friend Jeannie from Montreal understood how important these accomplishments were for me: *"Each new education certificate on the wall and advocacy award on the mantel piece healed bones and spirit, reasons to cheer her sheer determination to not only survive but thrive!"*

St. Clair College Graduation with Dr. Franklyn, myself, and Sister Emma

Part V

Transformation

"Transformation is a mystery that often happens,
not when something new begins, but when something falls apart."
Richard Rohr

A transformative metamorphosis occurs in the unfolding process. For me, I was becoming a renewed Kathy, spreading my wings just like a butterfly when it emerges out of the chrysalis. I began to accept the professional opinions about my strengths and weaknesses by listening to logic so I could re-frame my perspective. I was moving, slowly arriving at acceptance, integration, and better self-control. I went from seeing myself as a victim to becoming a survivor. My negative attitude began to change when I recognized there were 'impairments' that I could modify by rediscovering my resilient strengths.

To overcome the towering wall of adversity in front of me, I began integrating parts of myself I thought were loss to me forever as I entered another stage of healing, one of renewal. I began to realize that I needed to be willing to set a new course for my place in the world. Numerous issues had to be overcome but what I wanted most of all was to be able to return to a semblance of my old self and discover what I did have control over. My long-term memory had weakened and slowly, with the help of my psychologist, Dr. Franklyn I realized an array of choices were before me.

Discovery, Mediation and Litigation

Regaining full independence became an obsession. Normal environmental stressors and obstacles had to be navigated including managing my finances. Settling the collision claim with different people at insurance companies became major stressors, so I was grateful that my parents hired a good lawyer. Discovery, mediation, and litigation unfolded over a seven-year span with legal arguments presented by both sides. Financial insecurity caused years of stressful uncertainty that were crazy making. I suffered emotionally and mentally trying to deal with my extreme impatience as I waited for a peaceful resolution. I was entangled in a multi-level system and neuropsychological testing was an integral and necessary component in the process. I became quite good at answering the questions. When a sixth test was ordered, 5 ½ years after the crash, Dr. Franklyn stepped in to protect me from the stress being caused. She wrote her argument in a letter to my lawyer:

> *Emotionally, Kathy should not go through another assessment which outlines her 'deficits' and reminds her of her cognitive loss. It must be kept in mind that a psychological assessment of any kind is a quite intrusive procedure ... She knows the battery almost by heart ...In addition, an individual's motivation level has great potential to impact the results.*

Demands for interviews had to be met, generating more than 30 reports prepared by medical experts and other professionals over the years. Six weeks after my lawyer received this letter from my psychologist, an occupational therapist from Toronto employed by Rehability Occupational Therapy Inc. was hired by my car insurance company, Liberty Mutual. A three-hour In-Home Occupational Therapy Assessment was arranged. I understood that her job was to make a professional judgment on my ability to function independently. In an eighteen-page report, her summary statement began by identifying features of cognitive impairment due to TBI drawing on the fifth neuropsychological assessment:

> *The client sustained significant neurocognitive disruption as a result of her injuries and the neuropsychological evaluation reports' findings are consistent with frontal lobe/diffuse axonal injuries ...the client presents deficits across multiple domains involving attentional processing, verbal reasoning, constructive practices, verbal learning, cognitive set formation, memory generative*

> *naming (with) evidence of focal neural cognitive compromise related to frontal lobe dysfunctional and left hemispherical neglect ...indicating that the client's neurocognitive deficits would be considered permanent in nature.*

When I first received a copy of her report 106 days after it was sent to the insurance company, I was very disturbed at the slant taken. I was being viewed by medical professionals as a 'client' with 'deficits' that crossed over several domains interfering with the possibility of leading a productive and satisfying life. The interviewer's task was to further evaluate how I went about daily living activities by using a scripted interview and noting her observations. What I remember most about this lady is that she was 'by the book' and very impersonal. She never seemed to take her eyes off her paper throughout the questioning period and just kept writing and writing. I wondered if she was really listening to what I was saying.

The report summarized my pre-accident and post-accident performance on 25 specific tasks requiring cognitive and physical coordination. A number was assigned to the degree of being functionally independent noting how I used the adaptive equipment that were already provided. Since my crash, I found some of the household assistive devices helpful. I also depended on family and neighbours for support in some of the more difficult day-to-day tasks. I was unable to demonstrate vacuuming, washing the floor, moving garbage to the curbside, and shovelling snow. Under 'Physical Tolerance' she also wanted to observe me squatting and crouching which was impossible due to the injuries to my leg and balance issues. I did my best to accommodate her requests while following the advice of my orthopedic surgeons. Her summary statement reported:

> *The client demonstrates the ability to respond in a direct and straight forward manner to all questions ...frequently referred to either her day planner or written journal ...cooperative throughout the assessment process, but it is noted that she declined to participate in the assessment of her ability to complete vacuuming and floor washing ...The client declined to participate in the assessment of her ability to complete a full squat. In addition, the weather conditions (there was a mix of snow and rain that day) prohibited assessment of the client's ability to complete snow shovelling tasks.*

Becoming an Advocate

I was confused as to why she wrote that I 'declined' specific tasks without an explanation. She confirmed I was cooperative and accommodating for the entire three hours. I never refused to answer her questions and I attempted to do all the tasks that I was physically able to do. I also demonstrated the use of 'safety related assistive devices' that were provided beforehand. Beyond the medical and physical limitations, the psychosocial factors that affected my health and wellness were never addressed except in her opening comments. The solution to becoming functionally independent at home from this occupational therapist's perspective was providing additional assistive devices: *"It is recommended that alternate devices be issued in order to improve her performance further in completing bathroom cleaning, vacuuming ...It is the OT's opinion that Ms. Labbe should be capable of resuming pre-accident level of function within the home at all tasks."*

How was this possible when the report began with stating that I was faced with physical limitations and permanent neurocognitive difficulties? There were numerous contradictions and to this day I need to pause and deal with feelings of injustice that resurface. I was dealing with insurance companies and the fear was real that I was going to be cut off from benefits. I was also dealing with what seemed to be the never-ending court case. I was still meeting with my psychologist weekly, who made a note in my file on May 13th, 1999: *"Upsetting week. Anger is rearing its ugly head again. Frustration re: Insurance Company. Kathy reviewed the OT assessment report, and we noted some discrepancies and questionable comments. Kathryn will discuss these with her on May 17th."*

I believe it is one of the worse feelings in the world to be falsely accused under normal circumstances. People in authority who are entrusted to make expert assessments are a lifeline for economic stability. An honest evaluation has always been important to me. The power of words used in false accusations has psychosocial implications, so I left my psychologist's office with two questions that I had to think deeply about:

1. When I heard their point of view, what feelings are being raised and are they interfering with my ability to be open and rational?
2. Is it worth responding formally and face additional consequences?

Journaling and talking about this incident were helpful strategies in releasing the angry thoughts that were ruminating in my head. I had reached a critical fork in the road and had to decide which way I would go. I was trying to be rational and consider how the depth of my emotional resentment was affecting my reaction. If I couldn't fight back with the truth, I believed I would be distrusted, and the scrutiny would be never-ending. People with vulnerabilities can become easy targets for people in authority who have a different financial agenda. The sense of helplessness was overwhelming.

I have a certain level of satisfaction that I decided at this point in my recovery to be proactive. I channelled my anger into becoming my own advocate and composed what I considered to be a logical rebuttal letter (May 14th, 1999). I referred to the reports prepared by two different orthopedic surgeons (1996 and 1998) and used my voice to stand firm with my version of truth. Copies were provided to my psychologist, my lawyer, and the insurance adjustor increasing my confidence to give voice to my concerns. The occupational therapist returned the next week to discuss her findings and did not address my concerns or revise any of her comments. The following week, I met with Dr. Franklyn who noted: *"Kathy saw Ms. C. and presented her with a list of changes. To her credit, Kathy did not follow her impulse to throw the lady out of her house. She is concerned that the insurance company will cut off her benefits due to this assessment report."*

Dr. Franklyn also provided a rebuttal letter to my lawyer, supporting several discrepancies of which I was grateful. My car insurance company later approved expenses for training to improve functional performance in the tasks I had 'declined'. They also approved the purchase of a ridiculously long sponge to wash out my bathtub and a self-propelled vacuum that I could not use because it propelled faster than I could walk.

I was under intense scrutiny with a variety of opinions being made to settle the insurance claim. Thankfully, my long-term disability benefits from my employer's insurance company never stopped. However, I was routinely threatened by letters and phone calls that unless a doctor's note was received by a certain date my benefits would cease. I sympathized with the doctors being inundated for updated reports but the idea that I wouldn't be able to pay for my basic living expenses was a source of constant fear and anxiety. At one point my lawyer had to intercede on my behalf and remind the insurance companies that if they interrupted payments before a final resolution took place, a lawsuit would be issued.

Integration and Renewal

Medical professionals, as earlier cited by neuropsychologists and the occupational therapist predicted my 'neurocognitive deficits would be considered permanent in nature.' This prognosis was discouraging to accept. As much as healthcare practitioners helped me deal with the many challenges before me, I wanted to learn how to draw on my strengths so I could determine what more I could do to carve out a future for myself. In my mind I was questioning, "Do I just want to simply exist, or do I want to live a life with purpose?" Somehow, I knew I had to integrate the remnants of who I was, into who I was becoming. Adapting meant that I needed to set a new course for my place in the world. I recognized that I had numerous issues to overcome. What I wanted most of all was to be able to return to a semblance of my old self and discover what I did have control over. Accepting the fact that I was never going back to my life skills classroom took a long time because my identity as a teacher was so strong. There were suggestions by the neuropsychologist hired by the other driver's insurance company to return to teach at the elementary level that did not make sense to Dr. Franklyn: *"In a formal structured setting she is certainly aware of social niceties etc. However, this is one area of great difficulty. She is still uninhibited in her interactions. She certainly could not work with primary-junior children, due to her low frustration, tolerance, and propensity towards angry outbursts" (August 25, 1999).*

Brain Science Offers Hope

I needed the continued help of my psychologist to develop healthier interpersonal skills. The changes in my personality from TBI were dramatic so I had to re-learn how to control my angry, inappropriate, and irrelevant reactions. I was learning more about the discoveries in brain science. The ideas about 'neuroplasticity' has been seriously explored since the 1950s offering hope for recovery (Mateos-Aparicio & Rodriguez-Moreno, 2019). Neuro refers to neurons which are the nerve cells that are the building blocks of the brain and nervous system. Plasticity refers to the brain's ability to change or adjust. A remarkable function of the brain is the ability to repair itself because healthy nerve fibers (axons) can sprout new branches creating new pathways (Doidge, 2007). Importantly I started to recognize that damage was being caused when I reinforced negative pathways. I needed to consciously reroute my thinking by controlling my reactionary impulses so I could respond in a healthy manner. This was not going to be easy and 30 years later I am still learning how to accomplish this.

My thinking was changing as I became increasingly grateful for my father taking on the role of being my power of attorney. He was meticulous in obtaining and organizing my documentation, keeping records secure and submitting expenses. I needed to relearn how to trust that things would work out because I felt everyone was against me. I trusted my Dad and Mom, so I had to control my obsessive thinking about my future financial security. I concentrated on my breathing to slow myself down and practiced meditative techniques. I started listening to nature tapes of storms which reflected the chaos of my life. When the storm ended, I eased into the calmness created by the peaceful sounds of the gentle rain. I was walking with my cane in my neighbourhood and that also helped to ease the turbulence inside of me as I focused on the seasonal changes taking place around me. My senses were coming alive, and I was beginning to feel a deep appreciation of God's creation. The turbulence in my brain was being settled, even if those moments were temporary.

Pausing so I could slow down and use reason became a conscious strategy to change an automatic reaction to a more thought-out response. I was already exposed to the other simple strategies mentioned previously. It wasn't just one thing that worked but together they helped me adapt rather than react to the normal flow of daily situations. I just had to consistently use them. As Richard Rohr suggested, the process of transforming myself began to unfold when I realized that my world of being the old Kathy had fallen apart. Dr. Franklyn helped me stay focused on 'renewal' so I could recover the best parts of the old Kathy. There were many opportunities yet to be discovered if I was willing to take risk and put myself out there. She often reminded me to *"Do what you have to do!"* I had my driver's license reinstated by consciously drawing on the deep well of resilience that quietly rested in my long-term memory. Driving represented freedom and I felt that I had passed over a threshold to start making my own decisions. It was my ticket to get more involved in volunteering and participate as a functional adult in the outside world.

Volunteering

Improving my so-called 'deficits' so I could once again experience a sense of fulfillment really began when I started volunteering. I began to take advantage of opportunities that were presented, some I was successful at and others I realized were too difficult for me. Fatigue was a critical factor and I realized that using my brain and being emotionally present took considerable energy. When I was welcomed back to St. Anne's High School to supervise a small group of challenged students at lunch time, I really loved being there. A room was set aside for students to eat, work on homework, socialize, or play games. I also wrote a speech on *Traumatic Brain Injury* and presented it to a biology class. Being back with students made me happy but over time I felt sad as I could no longer relate to the teachers who had once been my colleagues. My world was so different from theirs. After a year, I felt grateful for the opportunity to spend time once again within the walls of my beloved St. Anne's community, but I knew I had to move on.

On Sundays, when I was up to it, I went to mass with my family where I found comfort being with my church community. I was one of the original founders of the Catholic Women's League at Our Lady of Perpetual Help and after they received word of my crash I was always in their prayers. One day I was asked to talk about my journey, and somewhere in my presentation I realized that each person listening to my trials and tribulations had a story of their own. Wisdom revealed that it was difficult at times to recognize the blessings hidden in the suffering. The experience fueled my determination to find a way into some sort of vocation that would draw on my teaching strengths. I was listening to the authentic truth in my heart and given a ray of hope to believe in possibilities once again.

Brain Injury Association

To help me deal with my wounded brain and anger issues, my brother Phil suggested that I investigate the Brain Injury Association of Windsor and Essex County (BIAWE). He believed I needed to talk to people who were dealing with similar problems. It took courage to overcome my fear of meeting new people. When I finally decided to go, I met others who truly understood what I was going through. I no longer felt vulnerable. Stories were shared and if I stopped mid-sentence because my brain would freeze searching for a word, I didn't feel judged. Together we rode the waves of turbulence in our lives. At times when I felt like I was drowning there was always someone reaching out with insightful suggestions from real-life lessons learned. Our support group is called, 'You are not alone' and it became a safe place to relate with others who are living similar cycles of never-ending frustration. Laughter and humour over some of the situations we found ourselves in became a release.

I took on responsibilities and became the representative for BIAWE for the Victorian Order of Nurses. I met Jan Tultz when I attended a workshop sponsored by the Windsor Coalition for Injury Prevention. Jan ran the pre-natal program and when she asked me to consider doing volunteer work assembling resource packages for their clientele, I felt two afternoons a week from 1 p.m. to 3 p.m. was manageable. When I first started, I found it hard because I became easily confused and tired. But as time went on, I became creative in finding a strategy of putting 80 packages together over a two-day period. I was having success and felt that I was contributing to a worthwhile cause.

BIAWE opened the door to many opportunities so I could learn and grow (https://biawe.com). Countless opportunities to participate in the many group activities helped me deal with loneliness and raised my self-confidence. I also enjoyed working on various artistic projects with others. The Butterfly Lane Alley Project between the roads of Argyle and Devonshire made the local news and raised awareness of TBI as the invisible disability (Saylor, 2021). My physical issues with eye-hand-brain coordination surfaced when I became mixed up assembling my butterfly on a piece of wood. It ended up with two detached wings - one was upside down and I placed the other sideways. When I stood back and saw the imperfections, I became very upset with myself. But when I paused and looked closer, I realized my artistic creation reflected my brain injury and it was beautiful just the way it was. Thank goodness for the pause!

Butterfly Lane creation with detached and upside down wings

New relationships entered my life. I continue to be passionate about injury prevention. Some people took a liking to my approach especially Debbie Boose who became a good friend helping me discover new things about myself:

> *Kathy and I met probably after my husband sustained a brain injury and we joined the Brain Injury Association. We became good friends through this difficult time, and she always spoke her mind. We gave her a name of 'Miss Attitude' but all in fun. I watched her grow as well as other people in the program who received the support they needed.*

I was seeing the value of sharing meaningful life lessons. I wasn't afraid to put myself out there, possibly facing disapproval for some of my behaviours. I was also willing to try new experiences. I was starting to believe that there was something I had to offer from deep listening. My new friends Tammy and Mike Filiault accompanied me on my journey and became forever friends:

> *When we look back at the early years after meeting Kathy, we remember her being focused and determined to go back to teaching young teenagers in a classroom setting but she hadn't realized she had never stopped teaching, just her students had changed at the 'school of life'. She chose many platforms to share her journey, from*

one-to-one conversations, support group meetings, to students in school auditoriums and to large audiences at provincial brain injury conferences. Kathy is a blessing, never hiding her experiences for there were highs and lows in the daily struggle to find her new "normal." We were lucky enough to be involved, as Kathy shared her road to recovery with us. We listened and learned.

I was pursuing my passion without a salary. I was beginning to understand that awareness and advocacy for the brain injured must occur at many levels for change to happen and I became a vocal advocate. Laura Kay was Executive Director of BIAWE when she asked me to accompany her to speak to a group of MPPs. We met to discuss rehabilitation funding for those involved in a motor vehicle crash and although I never found out the impact of our passionate plea, our voices were heard:

A few years after I met Kathy, my sister sustained a brain injury and I feel that I would not have had the knowledge or hope to help my sister if I had not met Kathy in my journey. She was an advocate and board member, and it wasn't long before she became a mentor and friend. She had first-hand experience, and I would say she is an expert in the subject teaching me how brain injuries can occur from crashes, falls, and even stroke. It took her years of recovering from a car crash to find a new path in life by sharing her story of learning, experiencing and survival. Kathy is very brave, and her self-awareness was inspirational to me. She was always an educator, and she continues to educate others to this day.

My dream of teaching was being fulfilled. I started to venture out more, accepting new responsibilities including mentoring others in the Peer Support Program. Serving as a mentor, I listen to others who are on their own healing journey, which is mutually beneficial. When I met Jeanette Ware-Mikhael, after she joined the Board of Directors, she told me she was good friends with the Sisters of the Holy Names of Jesus and Mary. We shared many heart-felt memories that reminded me to live life to the fullest by deepening my commitment to community service:

Being on the BIAWE Board comes with the responsibility of chairing a committee. Kathy and I partnered and were the co-chairs of the Social Committee. We planned monthly gatherings for those affected by an acquired brain injury. Kathy was a great partner and I enjoyed planning and meeting with her to brainstorm exciting ideas to engage all our participants. She would never hesitate to share ideas, help plan or attend a fundraiser, always bringing her Mom with her. She has worked very hard to recover from her car crash and continues to evolve and grow every day. I would describe Kathy as being passionate about life.

Ontario Brain Injury Association

I served nine years as a BIAWE board member, which is one of the affiliates of the Ontario Brain Injury Association (https://obia.ca). Each local group has their own charter and representatives who are invited to gather and share ideas throughout the year. At these meetings each affiliate can discuss their upcoming projects and outreach activities. Being self-supporting non-profit charities, fundraising ideas are also shared. An opportunity surfaced to serve as our local representative on the Advisory Committee for the Ontario Board of Directors. For six years I ventured out into the world taking the train on my own to Toronto for the Saturday meetings. I had to be super organized and overcome fear. One time I left my purse at the meeting, and I had to walk back to get it. I ended up with blisters that day, but the three hours that I had to wait for the train were very interesting taking in the sites of the busy city.

As a provincial registered charitable organization, OBIA is committed to enhancing the lives of people living with acquired brain injury (ABI). Training is offered through on-line courses, and I have been a guest speaker to share my experience as a survivor. My voice is still heard during the introduction to numerous modules in the Brain Basics program offered through Brock University (https://obia.ca/abi-training/brain-basics/). Sharing my story at workshops for different health care organizations such as Bayshore, Victoria Order of Nurses (V.O.N.) and Assisted Living Southwestern Ontario (ALSO) increased my confidence.

One of the big projects OBIA worked on was Drive Only Never Text (DONT). We had the Ontario Provincial Police stamp of approval, and they helped us promote our program with media coverage. Each affiliate of the Brain Injury Association also supported the project by promoting the message in their local communities. In Windsor, we developed a banner that was displayed in the main hallway at Windsor Regional Hospital, Ouellette Campus for one week. Every day we had volunteers hand out brochures, asking people to sign our banner. We gave them a blue rubber ring inscribed with DON'T as a reminder to avoid the critical risk-taking behaviour of driving and texting.

Mask representing the old and new Kathy

Unmasking Brain Injury

'Unmasking Brain Injury' was another major provincial project I worked on. The initial idea was spearheaded in the United States and a member brought the idea to our advisory committee for consideration. We worked out all the details for a year before formally presenting it to OBIA's Board of Directors. Twenty-three brain injury survivors from across the province painted a mask to display their journey, each as unique as their stories. The project was a huge success as the masks travelled across the province raising awareness about those living with brain injury.

I was asked to explain the project to our local newspaper's reporter Kelly Steele. An article was printed in the Windsor Star on June 24, 2018, with my mask. It has a bright yellow sun on one side representing my life before the cash. I saw my days filled with promise and believed I had a bright future ahead of me. As I began to let go of the old Kathy, I imagined myself as a ladybug who went into hiding to protect itself from the darkness of winter. Like the ladybug, brain trauma also sparks a protective mode and resilient tendencies can be buried deep inside. When I looked at my mask a year later, I found it funny that just like my life I painted the ladybug's antennas upside down. I still relate to the ladybug's courage to survive and thrive and even have a small tattoo as a reminder.

The PARTY Program

After one of my presentations, I received a phone call from Elsie Galbraith, the Director of Trauma Services at Hotel Dieu Grace Hospital. She asked me to think about being part of the PARTY program, which is an acronym for Prevent Alcohol and Risk-related Trauma in Youth (https://partyprogram.com). The model was first developed in 1986 at Sunnybrook Hospital in Toronto, Ontario and the main goal is to promote awareness and prevent risk-taking behaviours in youth. High school students participate in a mock trauma of a car crash caused by high-risk behaviours including drunk driving. Applying learning strategies that use vivid first-hand emotional experiences, the students imagine a scenario of a trauma patient who has made a risk-taking decision that would affect lives forever. Roles are assigned following a script that is evidence based so they become contributors of an ill-fated event.

Characters include an owner of a cottage on the lake who was not aware an all-day party was taking place, a youth who hosts it, friends who provide booze, others who stood by watching a passenger take advantage of a free ride home, and the person who left driving drunk. The students meet other 'actors' who weave their stories into the scenario including real life doctors, nurses, hospital staff, police officers, mental health workers, emergency service personnel, rehabilitation professionals, injury survivors, and organ donators. A practicing lawyer often attended the sessions to discuss the real-life expenses for the victim and the lawsuit for the plaintiff against the defendant to illustrate the crushing effects on the driver and their family. I was the real-life traumatic brain injury survivor who shared my story about the consequences after bad decisions are made.

It was hoped that the teachers who brought their students would debrief and talk about the life-threatening consequences of risk-taking behaviour. Over 100 sites around the world have adopted PARTY to increase awareness. I wasn't in a classroom, but I was being called to teach about risk taking with the hope that my real-life experience might make a difference in a young person's life. Combining reality in a hypothetical scenario influenced the students as presented in their testimonials posted on the website (http://partyprogramsa.org>testimonials). Interestingly, it was during one of the sessions that I met my co-author Dr. Suzanne De Froy for the first time. After three of her students from St. Michael's Alternative High School died in high-risk situations, she brought her class to experience the PARTY program. Many years later at a liturgy service I saw her again. I smiled and said, *"I know you!"* Who would have guessed a short while later she would volunteer to help me write my story.

It seemed like I had a lot on my plate, but volunteering was helping me get better and eventually I had to learn how to say, 'yes I can' or 'no I can't'. I also knew the importance of keeping a calendar, for my days were full. I had little time to be bored. I felt humbled when I received 'BIAWE's Mission Possible Award' and 'OBIA's Fellowship Award'. Volunteering gave me a life with purpose and helped raise my self-esteem. I received so much from people I met and couldn't believe that I was able to turn my tragedy into life-giving service. Brain injury associations are non-profit agencies, so I often volunteer at major fundraisers giving back my time in gratitude for all I received.

Volunteering at BIAWE Golf Tournament fundraiser

Dreams Turn into Goals

Having purpose to wake up and get out of bed generated feelings of contentment and gratitude. Volunteer opportunities became breakthroughs as intense anger was being replaced with empathy. Trusting the wisdom of my spiritual beliefs that still resided deep within helped me recognize the healing power of caring relationships. I became much calmer with fewer outbursts, and I was starting to believe that my life would get better. My dear friend Sister Helen saw my progress:

> *Kathy learned how to give motivational presentations to others who were suffering as she had from serious brain injuries and were trying to cope with life in new ways. She's a witness to so many others who struggle to achieve joy and hope again. I believe her success is rooted in her strong faith in God whom she somehow knew would keep on helping her.*

I have always believed that God is a Divine Spirit that works through people. During quiet moments in the early years of my recovery, I dreamed about driving and teaching once again. With help dreams turned into concrete goals and I worked hard to turn my dreams into reality. Driving gave me the freedom to be self-reliant and it was a major accomplishment for me. Teaching was a different story. I went back to high school and college to regain knowledge, but my good intentions had to be adjusted to life 'as it is', not 'as I would like it to be.'

I now realize we are all teachers in our own unique way because we each have the potential to lift one another up when we are down. This is the heart of volunteering. Beyond goals, I believe that my relationships were helping me regain my faith and spirituality. The positive energy attracted new opportunities into my life that were not a series of coincidences. As I improved, my third dream was having my story written down in a book. When I shared my dream at a liturgy service, Suzanne was there and offered to help make it happen. Her research background deepened my understanding about the complexities of TBI and recovery. Once again, I was able to feel the joy of a collaborative effort.

In April 2023 Suzanne and I were invited to present the empowering benefits of reclaiming inner resilience with members of Assisted Living in Southwestern Ontario. What an amazing feeling it was to hear voices chime in when the audience related their own story to what I was saying. We were encouraged that bouncing back from tragedy is a hope filled message, which became the focus of our presentation at the annual 2023 OBIA conference in Niagara Falls. Early in my recovery I recognized the special power of unfolding dreams when I wrote this poem:

I Have a Dream

I am a survivor because I have a dream.
My dream leads me toward the doors of
openness, honesty, and willingness.

I have a choice,
to shut the doors and walk back into
PAIN, MISERY, and CONFUSION
or come in tune with a new reality.

I choose survival, moving towards life
inch by inch
stroke by stroke
step by step.

The steps are so simple yet so very complicated.
One at a time
I can make moments of my dream come true.

Valentine's Day Painting 'Dreams do come true'

Part VI

Transcendence

"There is an underlying sacred worth in each of us.
It is deeper than anything that we feel at any given moment.
Even the most difficult feelings do not take away that worth."
Norm King

Healing transcends physical and invisible injuries by restoring wholeness. The impact of moderate to severe Traumatic Brain Injury depends on individual circumstances and is often characterized by long lasting cognitive, behavioural, emotional, and physical impairments. For those who have faith in a Divine Creator, their beliefs may be shattered. By moving beyond limitations and the wounds that bind us, feelings of unworthiness, inferiority, imperfection and failure are slowly released. After emerging from death's door with severe multiple impairments I became free from my own fatalistic thinking when I no longer accepted the well-intentioned and dreadful predictions made by some of my doctors and other professionals.

I have shared different stages of my journey at numerous presentations. The audience included survivors and others including professionals who tend to their care. TBI casts a wide net. After every session people commented on my incredible recovery. People who have known me for a long time find it hard to believe that I have come so far. My allergist, Dr. T. M. Liem has taken care of me since I was 18 years old, and my asthma was exasperated from the crash: *"I remember the day you came into my office with your Dad and Mom. You were very sick. Today you are a miracle by the Grace of God."* When I arrived at his office by ambulance, I was brought in on a stretcher with hopes to simply survive another day. The Grace of God unfolded in the many blessings I received from a compassionate circle of care. I did not walk alone on my journey to recovery for I was accompanied by many companions, and I will be forever grateful for their support.

The Silent Epidemic

My life has been especially enriched by my friends at BIAWE who truly understand what it means to live with brain injury. In my search for knowledge and self-awareness, I have asked myself many times, *"What more can be done to assist individuals and those in their own circle of care who live with moderate to severe TBI?"* Solutions for this invisible illness have been slow to emerge as it requires individual and collective effort across numerous domains. There is an urgent need for sustainable collaborative brain research as the statistics are staggering. A major international study conducted by neuroscientists predicts an annual increase in the number of TBI incidences. It is estimated sixty-nine million individuals will suffer lifelong consequences mainly due to preventable collisions (Dewan et al., 2018). This study determined systemic support for recovery varies from country to country due to accessibility and the gross national income level that funds healthcare.

The largest American study to date examined victims 16 years of age and older who received inpatient rehabilitation services after a primary diagnosis of moderate to severe TBI. After five years of being identified, the Centre for Disease Control and Prevention (CDC) posted the startling findings for the most severely injured who represent less than 10% of all persons hospitalized with a TBI: 22% died, 30% became worse, 22% stayed the same, and only 26% improved. In the concluding remarks, proactive policy recommendations recognized the need to designate 'chronic disease management' as a treatment model for TBI. This designation would recognize that changes are necessary to improve government policy making and aid decision makers in their planning considerations at long term and healthcare centres (https://www.cdc.gov/traumaticbraininjury/pdf/moderate_to_severe_tbi_lifelong-a.pdf).

In Canada hundreds of thousands of individuals live with moderate to severe TBI. Similar to the U.S. study, statistics reveal debilitating consequences that may affect a person's ability to function in everyday life. Support that is holistic in approach is recommended to prevent or reduce long term suffering and related issues that impact quality of life. The Brain Injury Canada's position paper, *Traumatic Brain Injury: A Lifelong Condition (2023)*, also recommended that TBI be classified as a chronic condition so improved policy can be created in health care for individuals, their families, and communities (https://braininjurycanada.ca/wp-content/uploads/2023/07/TBI-Paper-English-July-19-2023.pdf).

It is encouraging to see that the need to improve access to systemic support is receiving international attention for this 'silent epidemic.' Advocates for change are working diligently to raise awareness as the 'invisible' injuries do not mend like broken bones or damaged organs. Brain injury associations are non-profit organizations that reach out with numerous support programs for survivors and their families. Volunteers are committed to projects that increase attention for preventive measures such as wearing a helmet when bike riding. There are also numerous stories that are testimonies to the struggles that occur on a personal level, which can advance collective understanding on how to overcome adversity.

Each incident of TBI is unique due to the complexity of the human brain and related injuries. Personally, I can relate to Steve Bottrill's near-death experience after a car crash (2020). Steve's story is inspiring by explaining how he overcame his disabilities so he could begin living an 'extraordinary life'. He too had dreams. Steve believed in possibilities and achieved what others said was impossible. It was his passion that drove him to recover parts of his former self. He went from being paralyzed to becoming an aerobics instructor, from living on welfare to becoming a millionaire, and from the depths of despair he came to cherish his loving relationships. His inspiring mantra continues to resonate with me, "If you believe, you can achieve." Similar stories about recovering from brain injury were compiled by my friend Betty Penny in her book *Post Concussion: Brain empowerment (2021)*. She included testimonies from others who benefitted from BIAWE's non-profit activities, including myself. Our testimonies illustrate how recovery is a personal journey that becomes easier when accompanied by compassionate companions.

The car crash that caused my TBI brought chaos to my well-ordered and happy life. During the various stages of healing, I resisted the opinions from others to simply accept their advice, that *"It is what it is."* When I heard the words that my injuries were 'permanent' or that I would never walk again, I became more determined to find a way to improve my situation and not settle into desperate resignation. My silent mantra "Just watch me" became my own brand of self-talk as I faced the hurdles before me.

Happiness did come my way. On July 17th, 2004, eleven years after my crash, I walked down the aisle, without any assistance, into the arms of my husband Rob Worotny, the love of my life. I do not have biological children, but through our union I have acquired two stepdaughters and their husbands. I love them as if they are my own. They have blessed us with three granddaughters to love and enjoy. I never thought I was worthy to be loved so deeply and supported in the way Rob does each day. He never knew the previous Kathy and has been a witness to my daily struggles. His patience and non-judgmental attitude have helped him to adapt to brain injury in his own way, for which I am grateful. My long-time high school friend, Wanda Vanderveen wrote:

> *Years passed as Kathy rediscovered her resilient tendencies. With daily encouragement, she overcame trials with perseverance and bravery. Kathy continued to improve. Then came her wedding on the same day as her parents' 50th anniversary. There wasn't a dry eye in the church. By the grace of God, Kathy W A L K E D up the aisle, without crutches or a cane to her waiting husband to be, who has loved and supported her every need, with all his being.*

Our Wedding Day, July 17th 2004

The Inner Journey to Recover Resilience

Being empowered to improve from TBI as a renewed individual is viewed as a remarkable breakthrough according to statistics. Becoming self-aware of hidden resilient strengths has been a recent focus for healing. Years of research has led the American Psychological Association to acknowledge that resilience is part of the ordinary human condition, "involving behaviours, thoughts, and actions that anyone can learn and develop" (https://www.apaservices.org/practice/good-practice/building-resilience.pdf) (p. 1). At the present time there is not overall agreement on a definition that characterizes the many internal factors of resilience that contribute to recovery. However, there are promising results from research. Various components and strategies have the potential to help victims 'bounce back' from adversity and the resulting personality change resulting from brain injury.

Surviving a traumatic event is complex as the statistics illustrate. A major medical study was conducted in 2021 for nursing and healthcare workers and determined that the recovery process has received little attention in social-science research (Morse, J. et al). An extensive literature review highlighted different arguments as to whether resilience is a trait, a fluctuating state of potential, or a process of learning and adapting through experience. It has been my experience that all three perspectives are inter-related reflecting the dynamics of healing. A gap was identified in the practical components of resilience. Medical health professionals have tended to my care since day one and I appreciate that this group of health care professionals drew on the experience and wisdom of those living with illness.

Of the seven illnesses investigated in this study, I can relate to three: i) unexpected and unanticipated accident or trauma (car crash), ii) self- awareness of mental illness (anxiety and depression), and iii) exasperated episodic illness (asthma, chronic bronchitis, and leg pain). Each person interviewed in the study identified elements of resilience that helped ease distress and reduce symptoms. These included: acceptance, courage, knowledge, hope, humour, mindfulness, optimism, perception, perseverance, self-care, self-compassion, social support, and spirituality. There are different phases of recovery and throughout my thirty-year journey I can relate to each of these healing characteristics that helped me find my own way out of despair.

Building on the conceptual framework, eight other factors extend the practical components of resilience. Dreams, positive affirmations, information technology, healthy communication, healthy relationships, gratitude, forgiveness, and wisdom have also helped me move beyond my own pain and suffering. As separate pieces of the puzzle these qualities are interconnected and surface at different times in the healing process. I offer my humble understanding of these inter-connected concepts clustered under the sub-headings i) Fostering Wellness, ii) Building Connections, iii) Finding Purpose and, iv) Embrace Healthy Thoughts.

Fostering Wellness

Acceptance was the first step in adjusting my attitude toward the pain and suffering of my situation. I often cried and screamed after listening to the gloomy prognosis made by my doctors. The extent of my injuries changed my life forever but if I continued thinking that I could not bear to part with my old way of life, then I was not ready to anything new. It took years before I reached a tipping point and decided to straighten myself out so I could accept what could never be changed. As difficult as it was, I had to let go of 'who I thought the old Kathy was' so I could have the energy to push forward and face what was ahead. Reinventing myself meant I had to rediscover my strengths and believe in myself, despite being told over and over to just accept what many in the medical profession called my 'deficits'. I began quietly chanting, "Just watch me!" and a door opened shining the light of possibilities into the darkness of resignation.

Self-care means taking the time to improve my overall health. Certain areas of my brain such as my short-term memory are still problematic. When I realized that I was not taking my medication regularly I talked to my pharmacist who provided a blister pack. I was not afraid to ask for help. To reduce stressful anxiety, I like to have a routine. I have established a place in my house for everything and I stay organized by writing activities in my daybook. I am aware that moderate physical activity improves brain health and strengthens my body. I try to keep moving by using my membership at a fitness club. I also enjoy spending time in nature so a daily walk in the woods behind my house helps improve my mood. I enjoy cooking and as a life-time weight watcher I make healthy nutritional meals. I work at keeping my weight off so I can buy nice clothes that make me feel good. Finding what I enjoy doing and making good self-care decisions have helped rebuild my self-esteem.

Self-compassion is extending empathy to myself when I feel inadequate or foolish. It is being gentle with myself when I think I screwed up. I tend to

The never-ending journey of self-care and weight management

feel sorry for myself, ruminating over and over saying, *"If only I had a normal brain, that would not have happened"* and wonder if there really is such a thing as normal. Or I feel bad and ask myself *"Why did I say or do that?"* I need to regulate my impulses by trying to change the thoughts in my head. I call this strategy 'changing the channel.' I take the time to reflect on my intention as I would never want to hurt anyone. I also try to learn from awkward moments by accepting lingering limitations caused by my brain injury. By loving ALL aspects of myself I can overcome the deep sorrow of loss.

Perseverance is the 'umph' to get something done. I get a good feeling of accomplishment when I complete household tasks such as grocery shopping or finishing the laundry. However sometimes I push myself beyond my limits and I will become tired, frustrated, and miserable. So, it is important to be realistic. It took four years of pushing myself before this book was published. It was not easy, especially revisiting trauma and a very unhappy time in my life. My intention kept me going as I want to be a helpful advocate for TBI. My dream has come true, and I have acquired a deep friendship with my friend Suzanne. If my story can help others the effort was worthwhile.

Hope is a healing energy that was sent to me during a time when words had no meaning and comprehension was beyond my grasp. As I continue to improve, hope helps me imagine the way my life can be. It offers a light to see beyond the barriers that exist in the darkness of my own fears. When I am faced with a task, I need to quiet my misgivings and give an honest effort. Each time I am successful, I am even more hopeful that things in my life will get better. If I fail, I know there will be another way to get things done. One time in BIAWE's art class, we were asked to cut coloured paper into small pieces to create a mosaic picture. I had a hard time doing this task and I was cutting everything backwards. Frustrating hopelessness was mounting. I was just about to quit when the art teacher came over with a suggestion to fill in the outline with crayons and markers. I finished at the same time as everyone else and was very happy with a job well done. Finding hope in small accomplishments calms the turbulence and builds up faith, compassion, and empathy for myself so I can carry on.

Art class activity 'Adapting to a challenge'

Building Connections

Social support is relevant to every illness examined in the nursing and healthcare study. I agree with this important finding because I did not walk this journey alone. I discovered support comes in many different forms and sometimes from unexpected places. When I was ready to graciously accept support, I began to recover my self-esteem and self-confidence. When I don't have plans made with my family or friends, I can start feeling lonely and think about all the things that are wrong with me. Self-doubt becomes a debilitating part of a recurring cycle that I find myself in from time to time. It does not go away easily becoming a vicious circle that is difficult to break. Encouragement from others helps to reassure me that I am headed in the right direction.

Healthy relationships are the keys to survival. Interacting with others can be a two-way gift that is mutually uplifting. A longitudinal study tracked thousands of people over the course of 85 years and determined that embracing community helps us live longer and happier lives. Robert Waldinger, Psychiatrist and Director of the Harvard Study of Adult Development reported, "*The surprising finding is that our relationships and how happy we are in our relationships has a powerful influence on our health. Taking care of your body is important, but tending to your relationships is a form of self-care too. That, I think is the revelation*" (Mineo, 2017). In the early years of my recovery, I was in protective mode and lacked empathy. I was primarily focused on getting my needs met and I was less aware of the needs and feelings of other people. It was very difficult to accept Dr. Franklyn's diagnosis that I tended to be self-centred and egocentric that is typical with TBI. We often discussed how I could have handled different situations with more compassion. These honest discussions helped me slowly grow into self-awareness and reconsider disturbing behaviour. With each conscious act of kindness such as offering a smile or reaching out to lend a helping hand, I felt empowered over my brain injury.

Healthy communication is a basic human social need that connects us with others. Harmful misunderstandings often occurred unintentionally when what I wanted to say was not what I said. It is difficult to communicate clearly when my underlying frustration gets in the way. I work on avoiding assumptions, so I don't make *'an ass of you and me.'* I have grown more confident in being socially aware, so I do a 'perception check' to clarify what I am saying or what I am hearing. My body language can be defensive, and my tone can be perceived as demanding. I try to be aware of this tendency and simply relax the tension in my body. Sometimes I hear what is said as criticism instead of a helpful suggestion or an opinion. After practicing deep listening with other survivors, I began to recognize common protective defense mechanisms prevent me from seeing another point of view. I also need to deal with my expectations in a gentle and quiet way rather than getting angry or fly off the handle when things do not go my way. I have learned how to mend the wounds that I did not realize I caused. By accepting responsibility to work on the way I listen and talk to others I am tending to my relationships. I cherish my husband, family and good friends who challenge and accept me as I am.

Gratitude for the goodness in my life helped me reach a turning point in my recovery. I learned this lesson from my dear friend Sr. Emma when I was severely depressed in the hospital. We made a list of blessings that I recorded in my journal, and I often return to that memory. I use this simple reminder when I mentor other survivors. It seems to help them reframe their misery and suffering, even if it is only for a moment in their day. I often send cards that express gratitude just to let someone know how much they are appreciated. It takes time to recognize caring relationships are gifts that need to be treasured.

Finding Purpose

Dreams can uncover a purpose for living and restore a sense of meaning. A quote attributed to holocaust survivor and psychiatrist Viktor Frankl offers wise advice, *"Life is never made unbearable by circumstances, but only by a lack of meaning and purpose."* Returning to teaching was my dream that led me to volunteering. By listening to the whispers tugging at me, I took the risk to explore opportunities, not knowing where it would lead. It all began with small steps of sitting at lunch tables listening to the stories of those who were in the same shoes I was in. Later I was invited to share my journey as a guest speaker. Over time I became a mentor to TBI survivors and helped develop programs for OBIA. After a while, I came to realize that I did not need to be in a classroom. As I carved out a new place for myself in the world my life became meaningful once again.

Courage is risk-taking that comes from the heart so I could move foward and turn dreams into reality. A famous quote from poet T. S. Eliot offers inspiration to TBI survivors, *"Only those who will risk going too far can* *possibly find out how far one can go.*" There are times I am scared or unsure of my ability to take care of ordinary day-to-day responsibilities. Some days it is as simple as getting out of bed to face the day or get out of my chair and do something else other than watch TV. If I never face my fears of possible failure, I might never know the inner strength I have, or feel the power to overcome my insecurities. Getting behind the wheel and driving again is probably my best example. I really despised being dependent on others to get me around. I wanted freedom and that is what driving represented. With encouragement I pushed back against resistance to find out what it would take to get my license reinstated. Courage draws on inner strength so we can tackle mountains.

Knowledge is critical to understand how my mind works, what strengthens it, and what weakens it. I overcame deep resentment when I started relearning basic things that were previously automatic. I wanted to reclaim knowledge and went back to high school and then college. That decision was very humbling. My psychologist, Dr. Franklyn often said, *"Do what you need to do to get it done"* and when I finally walked across the stage at St. Clair College, she was beside me. Being open to learn has become a lifelong process. I seek out knowledge and inspirational wisdom to help me deal with my TBI. If there is something new that I need to do, I must slow down, not get frustrated and take enough time to understand. Since my crash there have been new findings in brain science that under certain conditions the brain can heal itself by creating new pathways when neurons have been damaged. Dr. Sanjay Gupta, a popular guest on CNN explains the medical side of things in layperson's terms. As the author of *Keep Sharp: Build a Better Brain at Any Age (2021)* he offers suggestions on how to think about our brains, how to care for it and how we can support its full potential. This is exciting news for survivors.

Information technology is a tool that helps me navigate an increasingly complex world. I want to keep myself informed about what is going on in my community and the world. I read our local newspaper that is geared to a grade 6 reading level. Devices such as audio and electronic books can be helpful to deal with auditory and sight problems. Kindle has built in a vocabulary so I can highlight a word and the meaning appears. When we went through the pandemic the zoom feature on my devices kept me connected to the outside world. There is always something new to learn about my computer, iPad, and my android phone. If I can't figure something out, I ask for help. I stay on top of recent TBI advancements by reading the OBIA review and Brain Injury Speaks that are posted online. Sometimes I listen to the news on the TV more than once to get the information straight in my head. Advances in technology has provided the tools that help my efforts to retain information. For fun, I like to participate in surveys and sometimes I get a monetary reward. Rebuilding confidence to share what I understand rather than sitting quiet in the background has given meaning and purpose to my life.

Embrace Healthy Thoughts

Perception is the way I see the world and myself in it. Norm King reminds me that *"There is an underlying sacred worth in each of us."* I had to overcome self-doubt that I was not worthy to contribute or live a meaningful life. There are times I doubt my intelligence and begin thinking I am not up to par with other people. This leads to the non-stop chattering that runs through my head making me stuck. This debilitating problem of ruminating negative thoughts creates doubt and causes me to be scattered. Confusion and a lack of confidence negatively impacts my self-esteem. If I am tired or overwhelmed my perception can get cloudy and messy and I can't think straight. At times I get blocked, thinking that the world is against me. Resilience surfaced when I realized that I needed to be the guardian of my own thoughts. I began to regain trust and started giving people the benefit of the doubt. By being open to listen deeply I can sense the intention behind what is being communicated and misunderstandings can get cleared up. My perception changes when fear melts away and I can feel the sacredness in another. This helps me recognize the sacredness that is also within me.

Humour is a relief to the numbness that can overtake my emotions. Living as a TBI survivor is filled with uncertainty and worry so I know that if I didn't laugh, I would be crying all the time. Laughing brings joy amidst sorrow. I try to be light-hearted and not take myself too seriously, which is easy among my friends at BIAWE. I tend to laugh at some of the awkward things I do or say with people who accept me the way I am. Our family has always enjoyed being a part of playful pranks like writing HELP ME on the bottom of my brother's shoes the day he was married. I was known at school for my playful antics by dressing up like a clown. I used that idea to make an outfit when I volunteered to bring a spark of happiness to sick children in the hospital one Christmas. When I can see the funny side of things, it helps me deal with the tough times by relieving the stress, anxiety and fear that can build up.

Kathy being a playful volunteer

Mindfulness is being present to whatever is happening at the time. Sitting quietly under a tree in my backyard and simply tuning into my senses has helped me become peaceful and calm. When I get nervous, I try to slow down and shift my focus to my breathing. When I think I'm being misunderstood I try not to be defensive. When there is a need to deal with a stranger's support, I remind myself to be calm so I can act like a reasonable advocate for myself. For example, when I had to call Service Canada, I was abruptly placed on hold for the next available agent. As I waited for 35 minutes, I told myself that I can get my message across, not get flustered, and not allow my anger to surface. I needed to control my thinking so I would not become disoriented and unclear. I turned to playing Mahjong to pass the time while I waited. Computer games can be a healthy and calming distraction when taken in small doses. When an agent finally answered, I was able to speak intelligently and with clarity - my problem was solved. There are many ways to learn how to turn inward and be mindful. It takes practice but worth the effort.

Optimism is having a positive perspective about future possibilities. It is a necessary outlook when trying to resist the negative thinking that keeps coming back. Tracy Miller, an employee at Chrysalis Day Club, once gave me a perplexed look when I was being very negative. She firmly asked me, *"Are you going to dwell on everything negative for the rest of the day? Or are you going to find the positive in what we are doing here?"* She was being honest, and I heard her intention. I have never forgotten the wisdom in what she said. Without seeing a grain of something good in every situation, I find myself being pulled down. I sometimes need a reminder to be the guardian of my thoughts. Otherwise, negative, and destructive thinking becomes further entrenched and a lack of motivation creeps in to overtake my spirit.

Positive affirmations that uplift my spirit give me a different way to think. Believing in the sacredness of life, that I had an important role to fulfill helped me to move forward. This was the mystery. In the six years I spent with Dr. Franklyn I left her office every week with simple sayings that I could remember. These helped me deal with my problems, such as *"Just do what I need to do"* or *"Don't give away my power."* I appreciate my good friends sending me positive sayings that can help soothe the negativity that still overtakes my thinking. To regain my resilient qualities and bounce back from the dark depths of despair means I will always be seriously looking at what I dwell on. To be able to experience joy and happiness also means I must assume responsibility to do the necessary hard work of looking critically at my decisions. If I am not being positive, I need to change my outlook and let go.

Spirituality is the compassionate energy of life and healing. It is the mystery of faith that flows into trust that something good can come out of a traumatic crisis. The nursing study we used to explain components of resilience identified 'spiritual health of an individual' as a factor in the healing process. Resources are being produced that acknowledge 'spiritual care' as an integral component in the overarching complexity of recovery (https://www.albertahealthservices.ca/assets/programs/ps-1026227-health-care-religious-beliefs.pdf). As a former religion teacher and participant in the interfaith movement I realize there are over 4,000 recognized religious and spiritual traditions in the world consisting of churches, congregations, faith groups, tribes, cultures, and movements. Common to all is an acknowledgement that suffering is part of life. A very wise chaplain visited me in the hospital and challenged my thinking by asking, *"Do you think that guy woke up in the morning and said, I'm going to destroy Kathy's life?"* Maybe not. But blaming is an obstacle of unresolved hurt that is easy to slide into. Compassion is the spiritual energy that has the power to quell the harsh inner voice and decrease anxiety, depression, anger, and loneliness. It is the spiritual connective thread that can help TBI survivors interact positively with the world and with other people.

Thirty Years Later

Many factors influence recovery from a traumatic event and cannot be reduced to one single element. It is hopeful to see that the medical community has been exploring spirituality as a healing agent. Steadfast love generously offered in my relationships became spiritual nourishment in my healing journey. I grew up in a family that believed in the healing messages brought to us by Jesus and devoted my life to spread his empowering love. Even so, for many years my faith was shattered because I blamed God for my misfortune and could not understand *"Why me?"* I also blamed the guy who ran the red light changing my life forever. It took many years to learn that holding onto hate is continued suffering. I had to figure out how to let go and turn suffering into something good.

FORGIVENESS was a major focus in many sessions with Dr. Franklyn who helped me realize that I alone had the power to release the invisible binds that wrapped around my mind and heart. She knew how difficult that would be. As a spiritual and resilient concept, I lost the ability to grasp the meaning of compassion. After I left her care I swept forgiveness under the carpet. I had too much anger to realize what her words meant. A new 'science of forgiveness' has generated two decades of research and found areas in the brain associated with forgiveness are deep in the emotional centres that lie underneath the temporal lobes known as the limbic system (Farrow & Woodruff, 2007). This is an area of my brain that was damaged and may account for the drastic personality change that I had to overcome. I am blessed that my immediate family has forgiven me and have stood by me with their unconditional love.

Making a conscious decision to think about my deeper values of empathy and compassion began to shift my darker moods. It did not happen all at once. Once I realized forgiveness does not mean forgetting or condoning the other driver's lapse of judgement, the anger was slowly released. I can talk about him today without emotional anguish and I no longer want to cause him harm. I have taken back my power, no longer spending time and energy on revenge. I have moved on.

My parents, Mary Therese and Romeo Labbe

Daughter Alisha, and her husband Brad with their daughter Emma (Parent); their mother Laurie Worotny; Daughter Allison, and her husband Jessy, with their daughters Lainey and Olivia (Amyotte)

My brother Phil Labbe and my sister Pauline Shurak

Canada's first memorial dedicated to those afflicted with a brain injury was presented to the City of Windsor in 2014 and placed in the sculpture garden along the riverfront. It is a reminder of those who have died from brain injury and those who suffer every day. A bronze sculpture depicting the release of two butterflies from outstretched hands sits on a five-foot granite base. Intended to raise awareness of the silent epidemic, the symbolism represents renewal. The journey from caterpillar to chrysalis, to butterfly represents the hopeful transforming journey of a person with brain injury. My husband Rob, family and close friends were present at the ceremony in 2019 when my name was engraved into the granite. My cousin Darlene Martell from Cape Breton has been a 30-year witness to my journey:

> *Kathy is like a sister to me. Since her crash she is still a fun-loving person ready to do anything at a moment's notice and at times she can be very blunt. But it doesn't bother me because I know her filter doesn't work like it used to lol. Our love has always been unconditional. Her confidence has blossomed since she started working with the people associated with the brain injury association and others she has met on her journey to wellness. Kathy's name is inscribed on the butterfly monument dedicated to brain injury survivors that is in the sculpture garden on the Windsor riverfront. She has come out of hiding and is spreading her beautiful wings.*

I have learned that transcending limitations to become self-reliant requires rediscovering hidden strengths. Reclaiming the power of resilience required three basic elements: i) wisdom to recognize what is possible ii) resourcefulness and creativity to improve impairments, and iii) self-care as working hard to reach specific goals. This is known in the medical world as efficacy.

WISDOM to imagine possibilities beyond limitations requires a change in perception and interpretation, which were skewed from my brain damage. Inner wisdom is deeper than acquiring knowledge or information. Commitment to change my situation and improve impairment meant I had to be resourceful. Turning dreams into specific goals triggered a renewed reality. It was not easy and required hard work. I often felt I was running a triathlon, or I should say walk as I cannot run. Change occurred at a very slow pace, and it will continue for the rest of my life.

When the fog of confusion started to lift, I wanted to be authentic and true to myself by discovering a renewed Kathy so life could become meaningful again. Writing this book, I stumbled on a prayer that we used

With my husband Rob at the Butterfly Monument in the Sculpture Garden along Windsor's riverfront

to start each day when I was a life-skills teacher that provided inspiration to everyone in our class, including me. The words give new meaning in my healing journey:

I am worth celebrating

I am unique.
In the whole world there is only one me
There is only one person with my talents, experience, and gifts.
I have immense potential to love, care, create, grow and sacrifice...
I am accepted, I am okay, I am loved in spite of everything.
So, I love myself and nourish the seeds within me.
Now is a new beginning, a new life given freely.
So, I celebrate the miracle and I celebrate me.

Dr. Franklyn helped to stir my memory of what was important to me and how resilient I was before the crash. I needed patience to go deep inside my experiential memory so I could rediscover my strengths to navigate the hundreds of choices faced in day-to-day life. As healing progressed, regret and guilt often washed over me as I thought about how I treated my family. Much too often, I raised my voice and yelled at everyone around me. It took time for them to understand when my brain injury was lashing out. It felt like a release from my never-ending frustrations and to this day I do not realize I am doing it. These are the times that I need to forgive myself. Whether forgiveness is a trait, state, or process, it takes time and requires both mind and heart.

I believe those who suffer are not forever doomed to be stuck in their injuries. Rumination was the greatest barrier in my healing journey, and still is. My assumptions about fairness and my place in the world were shattered, which is a normal response to trauma. As a negative connotation, a victim mentality is not easy to acknowledge. How we see ourselves dealing with the chronic outcomes from TBI is crucial to determine whether we can emerge out of a boring and debilitating track with a never changing daily routine. Negative thoughts that entrench a victimhood mindset can easily become part of a renewed identity, so I always need to be on my guard.

I often asked myself if I was going to be a victim or a survivor for the rest of my life? I had to adjust and take responsibility to tend to my emotional, mental, physical, and spiritual well-being as well as my relationships so that something good would come out of the suffering. With the critical insights provided by my doctors, I began to understand my changed circumstances, a critical step forward in acceptance. My general practitioner, Dr. Albert P. Ng has tended to my care since I entered the rehabilitation ward. We talked about my initial resistance to accept the effects of my injuries and that eventually he noticed a shift in my attitude:

> *Brain injury is difficult to deal with and there are various deficits with each person. By not accepting what has been dealt, a person will become stuck. You have moved on because you have accepted what you were faced with, and you continue to move forward. Acceptance is the most important factor in getting better.*

I believe every person faced with TBI or ABI is on their own journey to find a way to calmly cope with the many causes and symptoms of their illness. My hope is that other survivors will find their source of resilience as a way out of the darkness of despair, to not only survive but thrive. I believe rediscovering elements of resilience can become a lifeline to empowerment, defined by every person's unique personal experience. Victims and their families will have a multitude of career professionals who will cross their path. The conceptual framework of resilience presented in the nursing and healthcare study provides useful guidance for individuals and their dedicated circle of care.

Getting a second chance to be alive is a valuable gift so I try to make the most of each day. I have accepted the fact that brain impairments do not go away but there is hope for improvement. The rehabilitation phase does not last forever and neither does counselling from compassionate professionals such as my psychologist, Dr. Carol Franklyn. I have internalized many of her affirmations, which I often share with the brain injury survivors I am mentoring. During stressful interactions, I remind myself to pause when my expectations are not met. I have entrusted close family and friends to gently remind me of alternative healthy responses when old habits surface.

Every day I work at being flexible by taking the unexpected in stride. A noticeable change in my behaviour is the intense anger I hung onto for years has subsided considerably. I have curbed my tendency to swear, and I work on being kind by monitoring what I say. I have felt the uplifting freedom of taking responsibility for my life by standing on my own two feet and taking one step at a time. My neighbour and dear friend, Sharon Beneteau, never knew the old Kathy but is very aware of my struggles. When I asked her to share her impression of the renewed Kathy, she wrote:

Martin Luther King, once said, "I have a dream." Well, I say to you, "I have a neighbour. A real, true, honest to God, neighbour." She listens, she shares, she helps, and she looks out for me. She shows kindness and compassion to everyone she meets. Her wisdom not only impresses me but also makes me laugh because her insights are dead on. One day she shared an encounter with a stranger:

Man:	Can you help me? I need money to take a bus to Belle River.
Kathy:	But there is no bus to Belle River.
Man:	I have family there and I need to get there.
Kathy:	Well, call your family to come and get you.
Man:	I need money!!
Kathy:	Sir, I'll buy you food but I'm not giving you money.
Man:	F**k off!
Kathy:	Thank you!

That unexpected experience happened on a dark winter night when I left an appointment that was by the river. After I got in my car the stranger knocked on my driver's window. I locked my doors and opened the window three inches to find out what he wanted. After calmly saying '*Thank you*' I managed to pull away safely. I felt bad for his situation and wanted to help him yet at the same time, I felt proud of myself. I did not return his hostility or get flustered at his adamant request. I set a respectful boundary without getting angry or swearing back at him. As I drove off, I smiled to myself when I realized that his anger reflected a hurdle in my own journey. After saying thank you, I knew at that moment I was a survivor who was moving on.

Forever Friends, Kathy, Sharon, and Suzanne

From Kathy's husband Rob

When Kathy and I moved in together we needed to set up simple routines to help her memory such as putting her keys in the same place on the table. It was chaos when we had to look for over an hour only to find them in the fridge, right next to the milk. We can laugh about it now.

I can say that Kathy has done a great job adjusting to routines so things run smoothly in our home. I adore her determination to find ways to help her brain injury. She still needs to be reminded at times especially when she is under a lot of stress.

Thank you to our friend Debbie for introducing us. Kathy, the kids and I love you so very much!

A Closing Note from Dr. Carol Franklyn

I thoroughly enjoyed reading the book. I cried and I laughed. That this would be a challenging yet very interesting case, was immediately apparent. When I first met Kathy, she was barely able with assistance, to maneuver the stairs up to my office.

But there was a clear, defiant determination that exuded from her being.

In an instant, I knew that the potential for great success was present. Our journey together has been one of mutual learning and evolution. In spite of the serious challenges, there was also much laughter and fun.

I am honored to have been a part of her rehabilitation process.

Selected Bibliography

American Psychological Association. (2011, Apr). *Building your resilience.* https://www.apaservices.org/practice/good-practice/building-resilience.pdf

Bennett, H. (2022, Jan. 16). *Neuroplasticity: A neurologist explains how the brain recovers from injury.* BBC Science Focus. https://www.sciencefocus.com/the-human-body/can-brain-heal-itself

Biniarz, A. L. (2018). *Is your mind fixed or wired for growth?* The Drive Magazine, 113(9).

Bottrill, S. (2020). *The Steve Bottrill Story.* Petrolia, ON: New Dawning Press.

Brain Injury Canada. (2023, Jul 17). *Traumatic brain injury: A lifelong condition.* (Position Paper). https://braininjurycanada.ca/wp-content/uploads/2023/07/TBI-Paper-English-July-19-2023.pdf

Brain Injury Association Windsor Essex. (2023). *Testimonial by Kathy Worotny.* (YouTube) https://www.youtube.com/watch?v=g3FummpsxQQ

Centre for Disease Control and Prevention. (n.d.). *Moderate to severe traumatic brain injury is a lifelong condition.* https://www.cdc.gov/traumaticbraininjury/pdf/moderate_to_severe_tbi_lifelong-a.pdf

Dewan, M., Rattani, A., Gupta, S., et al. (2018, Apr. 27). *Estimating the global incidence of traumatic brain injury.* Journal of Neuropsychology. 130(4), 1080-1097 https://pubmed.ncbi.nlm.nih.gov/29701556/

Doidge, N. (2007). *The Brain that changes itself: Stories of personal triumph from the frontiers of brain science.* Penguin Random House.

Dossey, L. (1996). *Prayer is good medicine: How to reap the healing benefits of prayer.* San Francisco: HarperCollins Publisher.

Sherer, M., Vaccaro M., Whyte J., et al. (2007). *Facts About the Vegetative and Minimally Conscious States After Severe Brain* Injury. *The Consciousness Consortium.* https://msktc.org/tbi/factsheets/facts-about-vegetative-and-minimally-conscious-states-after-severe-brain-injury

Farrow, F., & Woodruff, P. (2007). *Neuroimaging of forgivability. In Handbook of forgiveness:* 283-296. Routledge.

Farrow, F. & Woodruff, P. (2007). *Empathy in mental illness.* Cambridge University Press.

Farrow, T. F. D., Zheng, Y., Wilkinson, I. D., et al. (2001, Aug. 8). *Investigating the functional anatomy of empathy and forgiveness.* NeuroReport, 12(11): 2433–2438. https://pubmed.ncbi.nlm.nih.gov/11496124/

Frankl, V. E. (2006 edition). *Man's search for meaning.* Beacon Press.

Gupta, S. (2021). Keep sharp: *Build a better brain at any age.* Simon & Shuster.

Health care and religious beliefs. (2015, Jun). Alberta Health Services. https://www.albertahealthservices.ca/assets/programs/ps-1026227-health-care-religious-beliefs.pdf

Jones, K. F., Pryor, J., Care-Unger, C., & Sipson, G. K. (2018). *Spirituality and its relationship with positive adjustment following traumatic brain injury; A scoping review.* Brain Injury, 32(13-14): 1612-1622 https://pubmed.ncbi.nlm.nih.gov/30182741/

Kathy's Story: *Overcoming the Overwhelming.* (2007, Fall). Chronicles of Caring: 15-17.

Kaufman, S. B. (2020, Jun 29). *Unraveling the mindset of victimhood. Scientific American.* https://www.scientificamerican.com/article/unraveling-the-mindset-of-victimhood/

King, N. (2022, Dec. 04). *A safe place.* http://www.touchingthespirit.ca/a-safe-place/

Konnikova, M. (2016, Feb. 11). *How people learn to become resilient.* The New Yorker. https://www.newyorker.com/science/maria-konnikova/the-secret-formula-for-resilience/amp

Loomans, D. & Loomans, J. (1994). *Full esteem ahead: 100 ways to build self-esteem in children & adults.* Tiburon, CA: H. J. Kramer Inc.

Mateos-Aparicio, P. & Rodriguez-Moreno, A. (2019, Feb. 27). *The impact of studying brain plasticity. Frontiers in cellular neuroscience.* 13(66). https://www.ncbi.nlm.nih.gov/pmc/articles/PMC6400842/

McAllister, T. (2008, Feb). *Neurobehavioral sequelae of traumatic brain injury: evaluation and management.* The World Psychiatric Association, World Psychiatry. 7(1): 3-10. https://www.ncbi.nlm.nih.gov/pmc/articles/PMC2327235/#!po=3.20513

McVean, A. (2019, May 31). *It's time to let the five stages of grief die.* McGill Office for Science and Society. https://www.mcgill.ca.

Morse, J., Kent-Marvick, J., Barry, L., Harvey, J., et al. (2021). *Developing the Resilience Framework for Nursing and Healthcare.* IN Global Qualitative Research. https://pubmed.ncbi.nlm.nih.gov/33869667/

OBIA Review. https://obia.ca/resources/obia-review-magazine/

Obonsawin M.C., Jefferis S., Lowe R., et al. (Nov. 2007). *A model of personality change after traumatic brain injury and the development of the Brain Injury Personality Scales.* J Neurol Neurosurg Psychiatry. 78(11): 1239-47. https://www.ncbi.nlm.nih.gov/pmc/articles/PMC2117599/

Okran, N., & Eksi, H. (2017, Aug. 04). *Spirituality in logotherapy. Spiritual Psychology and Counselling,* 2(2): 143-164. http://dx.doi.org/10.12738/spc.2017.2.0028

Ontario Brain Injury Association (n.d.*) Brain Basics in Person Training Programs.* https://obia.ca/abi-training/brain-basics/.

Penny, E. (2021). *Post Concussion: Brain Empowerment.* Published by author. https://www.amazon.ca/Post-Concussion-Brain-Empowerment-Happier/dp/B09LWP16ZY

Rohr, R. (2020). *The Wisdom Pattern: Order, disorder, reorder.* Cincinnati, OH: Franciscan Media.

Rohr, R. (n.d.) Richard Rohr Quotes. *Spirituality and Practice: Resources for spiritual journeys.* https://www.spiritualityandpractice.com/explorations/teachers/Richard-rohr/quotes

Sanford, A. (1947). *The healing light: The art and method of spiritual healing.* St. Paul, MN: Macalester Park Publishing. http://www.ezytouch.com/The_Healing_Light.pdf

Saylor, K. (2021, Oct. 2). *Butterfly Lane mural project raises awareness of brain injuries.* Windsor Star. https://windsorstar.com/news/local-news/butterfly-lane-mural-project-raises-awareness-of-brain-injuries

Segal, J. & Robinson, L. (2020, Oct.) *Volunteering and its surprising benefits.* Help Guide. https://www.helpguide.org/articles/healthy-living/volunteering-and-its-surprising-benefits.htm.

Sequichie-Hifler, J. (1992). *A Cherokee feast of days.* Tulsa, OK: Council Oak Publishing Co., Inc.

Slykhuis, T. A. (2014). *Starfish sky: Journeying back from brain injury.* Baico Publishing Inc.

Steele, K. (2018, Jun. 24). *Masked survivors help pull back the curtain on brain injuries.* Windsor Star. https://windsorstar.com/news/local-news/masked-survivors-help-pull-back-the-curtain-on-brain-injuries.

Sylwester, R. (1995). *A celebration of neurons: An educator's guide to the human brain.* Alexandria, VA: Association for Supervision and Curriculum Development.

SYNAPSE: Australia's Brain Injury Association. *Understanding brain injury* +. https://synapse.org.au/understanding-brain-injury

Unmasking Brain Injury. (n.d.). Mission Statement. http://unmaskingbraininjury.org

van der Kolk, B. A. (2014). *The body keeps the score: Brain, mind, and body in the healing of trauma.* Penguin Random House.

Weinstein, D. (2023, Feb. 7). *Loving yourself and others: The impact of compassion on mental health and wellness.* VCU Health. https://www.vcuhealth.org/news/loving-yourself-and-others-the-impact-of-compassion-on-mental-health-and-wellness

Wigle, J. (1995, Jun. 26). *Drivers Rehabilitation Services, The Hugh McMillan Rehabilitation Centre.* Document.

Wong, J. (2012). *Out of the Blue: A memoir of workplace depression, recovery, redemption and yes, happiness.* Canada. Published by author.

Wong, P. T. (2021, May 24). *The Frankl cure for the 21st century: Why self-transcendence is the key to mental health and flourishing.* International Network on Personal Meaning. https://www.meaning.ca/article/the-frankl-cure-for-the-21st-century-why-self-transcendence-is-the-key-to-mental-health-and-flourishing/

Worthington, E. (2004). *The new science of forgiveness. Greater Good Magazine: Science based insights for a meaningful life.* https://greatergood.berkeley.edu/article/item/the_new_science_of_forgiveness

Worthington E. (2020). *The science of forgiveness. John Templeton Foundation.* https://www.templeton.org/wp-content/uploads/2020/06/Forgiveness_final.pdf

Yang, Abigail (2021, Dec.) *Apprehending the Concept of Resilience: A Psychological Perspective on Resilience in Daily Life.* https://www.apa.org/ed/precollege/topss/daily-life-resilience.pdf

In Gratitude

In my 30-year journey there are many people who entered my Circle of Care. Without their steadfast unconditional love and support I would not be here today sharing my story. Dad was the meticulous record keeper who safeguarded every piece of documentation providing an accurate record of my recovery. He was my rock who tended to my needs so I could begin living independently in my own home. Mom did not drive, and Dad ensured that we were able to get to the countless appointments. He often waited with us to hear the latest update. Mom was with me every day while I was in the hospital and recovering at home encouraging me to "rise and shine." Their combined faith and encouragement helped me to not only survive but thrive. Dad kept tabs on the writing of this book and my regret is that he passed on July 12th, 2022, before I could hand him a copy.

To my beloved husband Rob. You are a dream come true for I never knew I would meet someone who deeply understands and accepts me just as I am. Your family has made us complete through their love: Daughter Alisha, and her husband Brad and their daughter Emma (Parent); Daughter Allison, and her husband Jessy, and their daughters Lainey and Olivia (Amyotte). You have all brought joy and happiness to my life.

To my siblings, Pauline and her husband, Eric Shurak, and my brother Phil and his wife Cathy. You were always gracious during my most cantankerous Moments. Your kindness and encouragement during my darkest hours have been the precious gift of family.

To my nephews Adam and Matthew Isherwood. Thank you for always making the time to help your Aunt Kathy.

To my extended family members who said many prayers: the Boudreau, Scanlan, Forgeron families on my Mom's side; the Labbe, Carter and Mailloux families on my Dad's side. You provided comfort during the darkest hours that helped sustain hope in my recovery.

To my cousin Richard LAbbe who is making a musical CD of my journey. Your creativity and love have always been appreciated.

To the Sisters of the Holy Names of Jesus and Mary, especially Sr. Emma who walked beside me during the darkest of days. You are part of my family. Your gift of prayers and unconditional love restored my faith.

To the countless nurses and medical professionals, many of you remain unnamed for privacy reasons. My physicians and specialists include Dr. Paul Barte, Dr. Albert Ng, Dr. Michael Hakim, Dr. T. H. Liem, Dr. S. Sanbourne, Dr. Robert Wilson, Dr. David Emon, Dr. Charles Hamilton, Dr. Frank Monforton, Dr. D. Fleming and especially Dr. Carol Franklyn who provided the light for my journey to wellness and endured my extreme highs and lows. Your care and professionalism helped me succeed on my journey to wellness.

To my friends at the Brain Injury Association Windsor Essex, St. Anne's High School and my church, Our Lady of Perpetual Help. Our friendship lightened my heavy burden.

To those who have given me so much encouragement and now rest in peace: Julie Labbe-Cooper; David Isherwood; Larraine Mailloux; Jimmy Scanlan, Carl and Loretta Boudreau; Bernard, Ed and Nick Labbe; Germaine and David Carter; Sharon, Mark and Lucille Forgeron. Silent prayers of gratitude are on their way.

To everyone who wrote encouraging messages in my visitor book and to those who were gracious in writing a testimonial about my recovery, including Jeannie Albert, Sharon Beneteau, Debbie Boose, Ann Boudreau, Joyce Carter, Mike and Tammy Filiault, Sharon Forgeron, Nicole Forgeron, Anna Jurak, Laura Kay, Marlene Landry, Dr. T. M. Liem, Darlene Martell, Pat Mulvey, Sister Helen Petrimoulx, Nurse Linda Proctor, Jean Tousignant, Wanda Vanderveen, Arlene Veitch, and Jeanette Ware-Mikhael. I will be forever grateful for your friendship and commitment to stay by my side.

Finally, to my dear friend and collaborator, Dr. Suzanne De Froy. You made my dream come true. You entered my life at a time I was ready to share what I have learned along my 30-year journey. You listened deeply so words reflect what rests in my heart. I can hear my voice and appreciate how you wove so many other voices into the pages of my journey. Brian injury does not go away. Your research skills have helped me become more confident and self-aware of possibilities. We learned together how to overcome limitations. I am also deeply grateful to your family and husband Bob Bergoine for the many hours you spent with me and the time you spent long after our visits were over.

KATHY WOROTNY

To my family and friends. You have shared my enthusiasm for this project and provided inspiration to persevere. It is true that undertaking a project that demands focused brain power will provide nourishment for the mind and spirit. Thank you once again for supporting me as I continue my own 'brain healing journey' in recovering from major depressive disorder.

To our editors and friends, Julie Lawrence, and Mary McNamara. Thank you for your generous offer to listen deeply. Your insightful recommendations in the final stages helped bring this memoir to fruition.

To our publishers Chris Edwards and Elaine Weeks at Walkerville Publishing, Inc. You have once again enriched our local community through your generosity. Your expertise in bringing this brain injury project into the final stages of publication is deeply appreciated.

To the many researchers dedicated to learning more about the brain's mysteries. Your discoveries are opening doors to possibilities into the many ways the brain is capable of healing itself. You have advanced knowledge in the mystery of healing and recovery that urgently needs attention. Your dedication and contributions offer possibilities to ease the suffering being felt around the world.

To Kathy. Writing your story over the past four years has been an honour. Your strength and courage to be an active participant in recovery is inspiring. Despite the many obstacles that came your way since that fateful day, you rediscovered your own resilient wisdom and never gave up. You have offered hope and wise advice, that the rate of improvement depends on developing an internal sense of self-awareness to better understand the changes that are happening during the different stages of healing. We laughed, cried, and prayed together as we went through caregiving, sickness, Covid, and deaths of loved ones. Your story illustrates that recovery is a personal mountainous journey with deep valleys and steep slopes to climb. At the same time, we cannot do it alone. As a collaborative project I learned so much more about the mysteries of the brain as we delved deeper into the research that reflected your personal experience. It is my hope that your story will provide inspiration, especially to those who suffer from brain injury along with their Circle of Care. We all face trauma and deep suffering during our life's journey. You have helped unmask possibilities so that a new and brighter future will emerge out of the chaos.

SUZANNE DE FROY

ABOUT THE AUTHORS

KATHY WOROTNY shared her story with supporting documentation collected by her family to writer and researcher Dr. Suzanne De Froy over a four-year period. As a collaborative effort, both authors have made substantial direct and intellectual contribution to the work and approve this publication.

Before her brain injury Kathy Worotny was a successful professional teacher with a Bachelor of Arts degree majoring in Psychology and a Bachelor of Education with a Special Education Specialist. She was a teacher supervisor overseeing an innovative life skills program. Kathy worked with educational assistants and teachers integrating students with mental and physical challenges into mainstream classes. The model was successful and used in other schools. Kathy was unable to return to teaching. She volunteers and continues to be a life-long learner. She values the support from her family to follow her dreams and lives in Windsor, Ontario.

SUZANNE DE FROY is a retired educator and curriculum designer who has worked on collaborative teams in high school, college, and university settings. Her Doctor of Education degree was earned at the University of Toronto in Human Development and Applied Psychology. Her research interests have included innovative and progressive problem-solving approaches applied in major restructuring initiatives including British Columbia and Ontario. Her recent interest in brain science, resilience and holistic empowering approaches to healing was triggered after suffering a major depressive disorder following the sickness and deaths of 13 family members in one year. She has been a board member and volunteer for numerous non-profit charities and has received the Queen Elizabeth Platinum Jubilee Pin for her service to family, community, and country. Suzanne values her family's support, especially her husband Bob Bergoine. She lives in Windsor, Ontario.

Manufactured by Amazon.ca
Bolton, ON

37338968R00081